Praise for
How We Love
by Milan and Kay Yerkovich

"*How We Love* has the capacity to change not only your marriage but every relationship that's important in your life."

    —JOSH MCDOWELL, Christian apologist, evangelist, and author of more than seventy-five books including *More Than a Carpenter* and *Evidence That Demands a Verdict*

"The authors have translated the complexity of how we love into a highly readable and clearly written book. Couples will easily be able to identify their love styles and how to transform them into genuine love. I recommend it to all couples."

    —HARVILLE HENDRIX, PHD, therapist and educator with over twenty-five years of experience, cofounder and president of the Institute for Imago Relationship Therapy, and author of *Getting the Love You Want*

"Milan and Kay bring us a fresh look at intimacy and how we learn to love. Their practical and personal approach will enrich anyone's marriage."

    —DAVID STOOP, PHD, psychologist and author of *When Couples Pray Together*

"I found *How We Love* to be extremely enlightening: a discovery of how best to love my wife, how to nurture her through a better understanding of our love styles, and how to implement change."

    —PHIL WAUGH, executive director of Covenant Marriage Movement

"I have had the joy and privilege of working with Milan and Kay on a professional level and have been amazed at the success of their therapeutic techniques. Understanding our love styles and taking down the walls created by our imprints are skills that can help every marriage. I am thrilled that more couples will learn how to strengthen their relationships through the tools described in this book."

    —DR. ELIZABETH JOHN, MD, psychiatrist

"Milan and Kay have taken their own life experience, their research over the years, and their experience in the counseling office, and distilled it into a work that is rigorous, original, and understandable. If you want to strengthen and enrich your marriage, as well as grow personally, I strongly encourage you to read and digest this material. The effect on all your relationships will be powerful."

—Dr. Jim Masteller, executive director of the Center for Individual
and Family Therapy

"Through Milan and Kay's candid stories, you will learn your own love style, find how to connect more deeply with your spouse, and ultimately realize who you were meant to be at the core of your being."

—Greg Campbell, retired business executive

"Forget everything external you think defines you. The quality of your relationships and your contributions to them are what make life great or miserable. This book is a key to a world of insight into intimacy only *you* can bring to your relationships. With each page, I felt Milan and Kay had seen my movie! My marriage is different today because of the simple, profound help I discovered in these pages."

—Kenny Luck, author of *Risk* and *Every Man, God's Man,* men's pastor
at Saddleback Church, and founder of Every Man Ministries

"The Yerkoviches have taken important developmental and psychological concepts and given them to us in a user-friendly fashion. They give us a peek into their personal journey and the countless people they have helped move from young hurts toward more meaningful intimate attachment. *How We Love* helps us see ourselves more clearly and understand our roles in the impasses of our relationships.… A practical and impactful read for all!"

—Jill Hubbard, PhD, clinical psychologist, cohost of *New Life Live!*
national radio program, speaker, and full-time mom

"I am excited that Milan and Kay have given us the guiding principles of a successful marriage. With candor and uncommon insight they have demystified the issues in relationships that cause so many couples to get stuck. This book will get the wheels rolling and provide a destination filled with hope, healing, and fulfillment."

—Dr. Mick Ukleja, president of LeadershipTraq and chair of the
Governing Council of the Ukleja Center for Ethical Leadership

Making Deeper
Connections in Marriage

How
We
Love

Workbook

Milan & Kay
Yerkovich

WATERBROOK
PRESS

How We Love Workbook
Published by WaterBrook Press
12265 Oracle Boulevard, Suite 200
Colorado Springs, Colorado 80921
A division of Random House Inc.

Details in some anecdotes and stories have been changed to protect the identities of the persons involved.

10-Digit ISBN 1-4000-7300-6
13-Digit ISBN 978-1-4000-7300-9

Published in association with the literary agency of Alive Communications Inc., 7680 Goddard Street, Suite 200, Colorado Springs, CO 80920, www.alivecommunications.com.

Printed in the United States of America
2006—First Edition

10 9 8 7 6 5 4 3 2 1

Contents

Part 4: Changing How We Love

How to Get the Most out of This Workbook

Whether it's a doctor's accurate diagnosis or a sudden revelation about a knotty problem, insight usually offers immediate comfort, but don't stop there. The important insight offered in *How We Love,* for instance, is merely head knowledge about the ways the experiences of our early years influence our adult relationships. And while the influences of our past can definitely help explain the difficulties we encounter in marriage, unless we're willing to commit to changing the areas of our lives that most need it, the information alone changes nothing.

Put differently, genuine change requires a commitment to growth. It means we will feel awkward, inadequate, and uncomfortable. It means we will have to work hard. It means we will have to fight against our resistance to change. The alternative, though, is to remain stuck right where we are in our relationships. And, folks, that is painful too. Either way, we'll experience discomfort and distress. Why not choose constructive discomfort? That's what we're offering in this workbook: the experience of constructive, beneficial discomfort! The trade-off of current uneasiness for the awkward pain of growth is the promise of future relief. In fact, in this book you will find hope for new levels of emerging security, trust, and intimacy in your marriage as well as healing from your injured love style. This love style, or imprint of intimacy, which was learned in your family of origin, has been controlling you for many years, and for most of us, it has adversely affected our capacity to successfully give and receive love.

The instruction in this workbook is all about improving your primary human relationship, your connection to your spouse. Although you'd certainly benefit from using this workbook on your own, we've intentionally designed it to be most useful for couples. There are also specific exercises for a group setting. Applying these insights in relationship is the only way to truly change how you love. Groups not only help you feel less alone in your struggles, they also provide encouragement and support as you hear other people's similar—and contrasting—experiences. Some questions may be distressing, so having your small group's support throughout this process will help you feel less overwhelmed. A small group can also encourage you to process your feelings and thoughts as you grow and change. The added bonus of accountability is that someone will know whether you complete the assignments and can help you persevere on the path of change.

You may find this workbook a bit different from others. Some pages—even some questions—will require more than a week to cover. That's okay! Give yourself the time you need to thoughtfully consider your answers. The time you spend reflecting on and evaluating your personal imprint, the core pattern of your marriage, and your progress toward change, is time well spent. Whether you work through this book with your spouse, a small group, or even alone, you will only grow and change according to the time and effort you put into answering the questions. There is much to discover about how you love, so be patient and know that real growth takes time. This workbook will be a good guide, but *you* are responsible for your own growth. We've intended for you to use this workbook along with a journal to record your thoughts and feelings as you interact with the questions. You may also find that you have different and surprising answers after you've gone through the exercises several times. That's a sign of growth!

If you are currently single, consider holding off on a new relationship until you can complete the exercises and develop the new habits in this workbook. Not only will you gain insights into your ability to choose an emotionally healthy mate, you will also acquire new levels of awareness that will help you become a better mate.

If your spouse is resistant to going through the material with you, forge ahead alone. In time, your new understanding and skills will have an effect upon your core pattern and will likely begin to gain your spouse's attention. Change yourself and see what happens.

Christian leaders take heart. Estimates show that one in three Christian leaders finishes well, yet the courage that brought you where you are right now will serve as you invest in these tools and learn to resist the gradual erosion of your marriage as you serve the Lord.

As you look intently at your past and present relationships, you may experience uncomfortable levels of emotional distress. If you feel overwhelmed and find yourself struggling to know how to handle your feelings, it is important that you call a professional therapist. As that person walks alongside you for a season, he or she will be familiar with the questions and personal reflection we have suggested in this book and will bring a measure of security to you and your spouse. There is also low-cost help available through local county programs, churches, and nonprofit organizations. Our sincere hope and prayer is that you'll stay motivated to continually dig deeper into your past as you begin to see positive changes from your efforts. This book and workbook are our personal journey. Believe us, the work is worth it! Make the investment in yourself and your marriage so you can indeed *finish well*. God bless you on your journey!

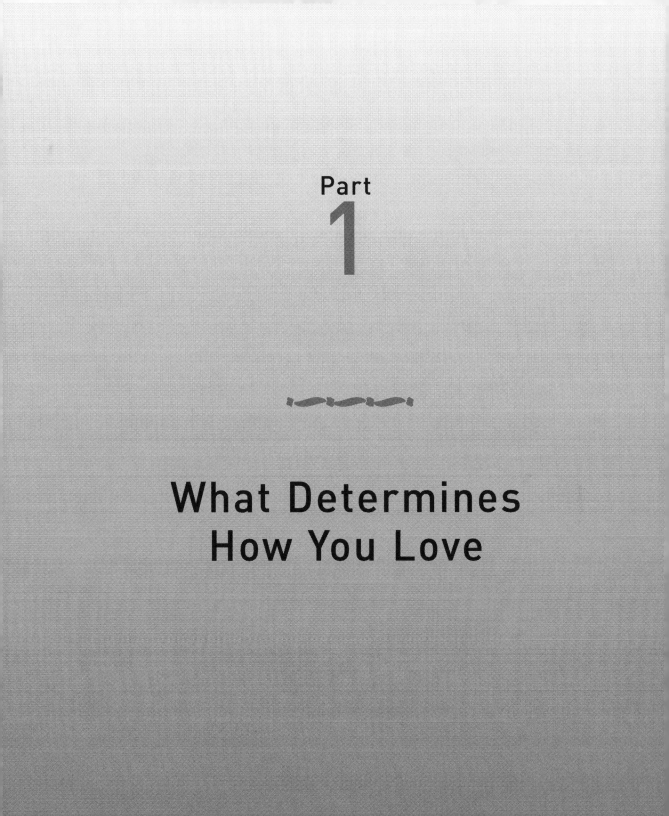

Part

1

What Determines How You Love

Why Every Marriage Gets Stuck

1. In chapter 1 we talked about nagging problems that grab our attention and keep us from getting to the roots of problems. Perhaps you are like us and have made symptoms the focal point of your efforts to improve your marriage. Describe some of the chronic irritations and patterns that remain unresolved.

2. We shared two truths in chapter 1. The first was that the close proximity of your partner triggers old feelings because you look to your spouse to meet some of the same needs your parents were supposed to meet. That means your marriage problems did not start in your marriage. What bothers you most about your spouse is undoubtedly related to painful experiences from his or her childhood or to the lack of training that would have prepared your mate and you to face the challenges of marriage. Without accusing or blaming, write down which of your spouse's attitudes or behaviors bothers you most.

3. What is your spouse's biggest complaint about you? Ask him or her if you're not sure.

4. The second truth in chapter 1 is this: you will never truly know yourself or your mate until you understand how each of you was shaped by your childhood experiences. Write about and discuss some key memories (especially relational hurts) that might relate to or have been the cause of the irritating traits you just wrote about.

Now take some time to write your answers to the following questions. These answers may help you better determine what is at the root of your marriage problems.

5. Do you fight about the same old subject over and over? Identify the topic and describe the usual fight. What are each partner's behaviors and beliefs?

6. Jot down any insights about how childhood wounds may be at the root of the behaviors and beliefs that fuel repetitive problems. (If this is too challenging, don't worry, as there is help ahead.)

7. A great starting place for our journey is the prayer Jesus prayed for you in John 17. Look at verses 20–23. What does Jesus pray for you? Now list the three or four most important relationships in your life today. Evaluate each of these relationships in light of this prayer.

8. Read Psalm 139:23–24. "Wicked way in me" (KJV), "offensive way in me" (NIV), and "hurtful way in me" (NASB) is literally in the Hebrew, according to the NASB notes, "way of pain." This workbook will help you identify specific ways of pain that hinder the expression of love and unity in your relationships. What ways of pain do you see in yourself and those you are in relationship with (the people you listed in question 7)?

9. God is capable of using far more than this workbook to help you experience and manifest his love in your relationships. Consider writing a personal prayer based on the ideas expressed in these verses, asking God to reveal new insights about the ways in which you give and receive love.

To follow are some statements that will help you evaluate the strengths and weaknesses in your marriage. Both you and your mate can respond by writing after each sentence a *Y* for *Yes* or an *NI* for *Needs Improvement.* Then use the inventory as a springboard for discussion.

Acceptance

_____ My mate knows my strengths and weaknesses, and I am fully accepted in spite of my shortcomings.

_____ I know my mate's strengths and weaknesses and fully accept him/her in spite of the shortcomings.

_____ When I make a mistake, my mate forgives me.

_____ When my mate makes a mistake, I forgive him/her.

Safety and Communication

_____ I feel safe to discuss any subject with my mate.

_____ I feel safe to share my deepest feelings, even my negative emotions.

_____ I am honest with my mate.

_____ My mate and I discuss sexual problems as they arise in our relationship.

_____ I can effectively communicate with my spouse about areas of disagreement and conflict.

_____ We usually reach resolution or compromise when we disagree about a problem.

_____ I am aware of my feelings and needs, and I communicate them.

_____ I try to understand the feelings and needs of my spouse and then respond to the feelings and meet the needs.

_____ My spouse and I pray together.

Support and Respect

_____ I feel that my mate sees, values, supports, and respects my uniqueness as a person.

_____ My mate knows my gifts and talents and encourages me to use them.

_____ I know my mate's gifts and talents, and I encourage him/her to use them.

Nurture and Comfort

_____ I receive comfort from my spouse when I need it.

_____ My spouse is able to receive comfort from me.

_____ We show affection and touch each other without the closeness necessarily becoming sexual.

Individuality and Space

_____ I have interests, hobbies, and friends apart from my mate.

_____ My mate has friends, hobbies, and interests outside our relationship.

_____ My spouse supports my participation in these pursuits and sees them as a healthy complement to couple/family time.

_____ I support my spouse's participation in these pursuits and see them as a healthy complement to couple/family time.

Fun and Play

_____ I have fun with my mate.

_____ We have regular time alone without kids or business distractions.

_____ We enjoy at least one recreational activity together.

_____ We laugh together.

_____ Most of the time we have an enjoyable sex life together.

Most of us have endured an annual review at work, that sometimes nerve-racking conversation during which our performance for the year is evaluated and ideas for improvement are discussed. A review can often spark important change, yet rarely do we take the time to do an annual review of the most important area of our lives: our marriages. But you've just reviewed your marriage as you've thought about many aspects of your relationship. Perhaps your list of items that need improvement is overwhelmingly long. If that's true, don't be discouraged before you even begin. Creating a healthy, satisfying marriage is worth the effort, and every step of growth moves you toward that goal.

One of the most important aspects of marriage—and a good habit to develop—is to have fun together as a couple. A mutual agreement to schedule date nights with the following guidelines can bring renewal and hope to a tired or taxed relationship.

GUIDELINES FOR FUN AND RENEWAL

- At the beginning of each month, schedule two date nights and put them on the calendar.
- Each partner is responsible for planning one of the dates. Decide when you mark your calendar who will plan the first date and who will plan the second.
- Date nights are for fun and enjoyment. *No problems will be discussed.*
- Use date-night conversations for praise, compliments, words of appreciation, and the sharing of good memories.

So get your calendars out now. Even if it's the middle of the month, plan a date—or even two.

The Revealing Question You Need to Answer

In chapter 2, we asked you to think about childhood memories of being comforted, and we discussed the ingredients of emotional connection between parents and children. We also considered the importance of learning to become aware of what's inside our hearts and of having soul words to describe our experiences.

You may think you are already familiar with the topic and acquainted with all you need to know. However, since it's this imprint of intimacy that affects your capacity to give and receive love, we believe the following questions may improve your ability to determine your love style.

Before you begin reviewing your history, we want to acknowledge that some of these questions may be difficult to answer, so just do your best. Asking relatives for their memories and insights is sometimes helpful, but that's up to you. Also, reflecting on your childhood experiences might be painful as you recall specific events. We feel it is very important for you to have a safe place to discuss your responses to these questions. Ideally, we hope you will be able to talk with your spouse. If that isn't possible, we recommend that you join a support group in which you can share what you're learning and process the feelings that arise. If you feel depressed or overwhelmed, please get some individual counseling before you continue these workbook exercises.

1. Do you have a memory of being comforted? If so, describe the scene—who was comforting you, why you needed comfort, and how effective that person's comfort was. Then evaluate the comfort you received in light of the three critical ingredients of comfort found on pages 15–17 of *How We Love*.

2. What comfort did each parent offer you in the following categories? Be as specific as possible.

Touch and Affection

Listening to You Talk and Responding with Insightful Questions

Validating Your Feelings

Addressing and Resolving Conflict

3. List the immediate family members you were consistently around as a child. Start with the most influential caregiver in your life (usually a parent), the second most influential, and then on through the other significant figures from your childhood. Next to each person's name, write the following:

- five descriptive words that reflect their personality and character
- three soul words that describe what you most often felt in the presence of that person (see the soul words list at the end of this book)
- your best memory of each person
- your worst memory of each person

4. If you could change one thing about your most influential caregiver, what would it be? What traits, if any, about this person did you enjoy?

5. If you could change one thing about your second most influential caregiver, what would it be? What traits, if any, about this person did you enjoy?

6. Think about people other than your biological parents who influenced your life, such as stepparents or grandparents. If you could change one thing about them, what would it be? What traits, if any, about these people did you enjoy?

7. Describe how your family handled feelings as you were growing up. Focus on the emotions of anger, sadness, fear, jealousy, and joy. What did your family do to encourage or discourage the expression of a variety of feelings? Be specific.

8. Which feelings did your family allow and perhaps even encourage?

9. Which feelings were simply not allowed?

10. Was any family member allowed to express feelings that other members were denied? Be specific about the family member and the feeling(s).

11. Are you currently able to appropriately express a variety of feelings? Explain. Which feelings, for instance, are acceptable, and which are not? Who in your life is a safe person for you to share feelings with, and who is not?

12. In chapter 2, we talked about soul words. Did your parents enable you to develop the skill of talking about your feelings? If not, know that it isn't too late. What steps can you take to learn this skill now?

13. Did anything in your home make you feel unsafe when you were growing up? What did you do to protect yourself?

14. Did any family members have addictions? Who was addicted to what? In what ways did this addiction affect the family? What impact did the addiction have on you?

15. We live in an imperfect world, and no parent is perfect, so all of us bring issues into our marriages. Psalm 139, however, gives us a picture of connection that serves as a blueprint for intimacy. Read that psalm and underline the words and phrases that you find most significant. Why do you think you respond to those ideas?

God created us with a need for emotional connection with Him and with other people. It was His idea that we should desire love, and He satisfies that desire by lovingly reaching out to us, watching over us, and guiding us, and by giving us relationships with other human beings. God, however, is our perfect parent, but since none of us had a perfect earthly parent, it is hard for us to understand exactly what that description means. For starters, it means that God knows our heart of hearts; He is intimately acquainted with us. When we embrace such attentive love—a love that guides and protects—we can more easily avoid the paths that lead to pain.

Now, having spent time thinking about Psalm 139, write your own psalm or paragraph describing your relationship with your parents. You may want to begin with "Dear Mom and Dad." *But do not give it to them.* The goal is not to assign blame or seek amends but to take an honest look at the things that hurt us when we were younger so that we can grow and change. The purpose is to zero in on what your emotional connection with your parents was like and then set some specific goals for your relationship with your spouse. If you've struggled to accept and trust in God's love as well as your spouse's love, this exercise may help you begin to understand why.

After you've written your own composition to your parents, consider sharing it with your spouse. Also discuss with someone safe (ideally your spouse) the impact your experience with your parents has had on your ability to experience intimacy with God and with your spouse.

16. Take turns sharing what thought, insight, or workbook question was most meaningful from this chapter.

Chapter 3

Imprints of Intimacy from Our First Lessons in Love

I n the preceding chapter of the workbook, you began seeing your childhood experience in a realistic light. As you continue with that exercise, remember that any time you read something new, that idea might serve as a good springboard for discussion with your spouse. Also, if using soul words is new to you, talking about your reactions to and thoughts about what you read will give you opportunities to practice. You might also copy the list of soul words at the back of this book and hang it on your refrigerator as a handy reference.

Review the meaning and characteristics of *implicit* and *explicit* memories on page 26 of *How We Love*. Remember how Tina's implicit memories affected her relationships? You might be wondering, *How am I supposed to remember anything from the first three or four years of my life?* In fact, most people can't remember early trauma but may have been told stories about such events. All of us have plenty of explicit memories from later years to draw from, which is the focus of the workbook. One of the reasons we included the story about Tina is because some people have always known about events or circumstances that occurred in childhood but never considered their impact on the way they relate.

1. If you know about a traumatic event during the first four or five years of your childhood, write about feelings and responses you may have experienced in the space below. Do you experience similar feelings in your current relationships? What triggers them?

2. Do you identify with Lee's struggle? Why do you think people are resistant to looking at their pasts? Are you struggling with this as well? Write down some of your thoughts and share them with your spouse.

3. You have to know yourself before you can change yourself. Why can taking a realistic look at your past help you know yourself better?

4. Take time to think about and talk about memories from your early years. Use the soul words list to express the feelings you experienced during the memory you are describing. If you like, you might also try stretching out on the couch and putting your head in your spouse's lap as you share. Write down the memory and the words you used to describe it in the space below.

UNDERSTANDING THE ROLES WE PLAYED

Relational experiences from our childhoods become wired into our behaviors and beliefs, and this is how it happens: When we were young and events or people hurt us, we used certain strategies to protect ourselves from those painful experiences. Somewhere along the way, for instance, we learned to play certain roles in an attempt to lessen tensions in the family. Over time those roles became a part of who we are, and they often operate without our awareness.

Just like old and familiar songs buried in the dusty attic of our minds, these childhood roles stay with us.

Children begin playing roles to gain attention, reduce disharmony, conform to parental expectations, or meet the needs of a parent. Look through the list below and see if any of these roles feel familiar.

- *Good Kid:* I made sure not to burden my parents.
- *Clown:* I used humor to reduce conflict and stress.
- *Invisible One:* I tried to avoid conflict and stress by hiding.

EXTRAORDINARY CHALLENGES

Difficult circumstances—severe loss, childhood trauma, family crises—can disrupt the process of bonding with one's parents, especially if you didn't have any opportunities to talk about what happened or express your negative feelings. And unless you had many opportunities as a child to express what was on your heart, you will struggle as an adult to process stressful situations and manage the accompanying feelings.

If any of the experiences listed below were a part of your history and you *did* have many opportunities to be listened to and comforted, their negative impact was probably greatly reduced. If no one was available to listen to you or comfort you, though, the negative impact might be significant. Either way, write about your experience and the impact you think it has had on you.

The following list isn't exhaustive, and you may remember some events not listed below that had a big effect on your family. Whatever those circumstances, consider their impact on you, especially on your ability to form close connections with others. Afterward, take time to share your observations and feelings with your spouse and/or small group.

"My parent was ill, or a sibling had serious health problems."
When someone in the home suffers from a serious illness, it adds tremendous stress to the family unit and may limit the time and energy available for parenting.

(continued on the next page)

"One of my parents died when I was growing up."

The death of a parent at any stage of a child's development is a horrendous trauma. What impact do you think this event had on your ability to form emotional connections with people?

"One of my parents was depressed or suffered from mental illness."

Brain damage, chemical imbalances, and psychological problems in a parent can negatively affect everyone else in the home. "Baby blues" are common after childbirth, but this usually dissipates within two weeks. However, a few new mothers experience more serious postpartum depression up to one year after childbirth. This is a serious condition that requires medical treatment and can definitely impact a family. (If you recognize symptoms of depression or mental illness in yourself or another family member, please seek medical help very soon. There are ways to alleviate suffering and stop the damage to your family, but you must choose to take action.)

"I've been told I was a fussy baby and cried all the time."

Some children are born with a hypersensitive nervous system and experience touch, sounds, lights, and smell as overwhelming, irritating, and overstimulating. As a result, they may have difficulty associating touch with pleasure and relief.

"My parent(s) had a hard time accepting my personality."

Parents may find they have personality conflicts with one of their children. (By the way, this kind of conflict seems to most often occur between the firstborn child and the same-sex parent.) Constant tension and discord can certainly impact bonding. Also, we've found that many adults who identify themselves as introverts believe they were not understood by their parents.

"I'm adopted."

Babies begin connecting to their mothers while they are still in the womb. They recognize their mothers' voices and even their intonations and rhythms. Although adoption is a wonderful alternative for mothers who are unable to keep their babies, it does interrupt the natural process of bonding.

"There were more than five kids in my family when I was growing up."

In very large families, parents are often consumed with meeting their children's basic needs. Consequently, Mom and Dad may be overwhelmed by the amount of work and therefore have little time to notice or attend to each child's emotional needs.

"My parents were busy all the time."

Perhaps you suffered from neglect, spent significant time in day care, or were largely raised by someone other than your parents.

"A sibling mistreated me."

Maybe an older brother or sister tormented you when your parents were not around. Perhaps they threatened you with serious consequences if you told your parents.

"I had medical problems when I was born or a serious illness as I was growing up."

Medical treatment during infancy or the preschool years can be problematic as children learn to associate touch with invasive and painful medical procedures. At times these children often feel great levels of distress that cannot be reduced by even the best parenting. (A high tolerance for pain is often an indicator of early physical or medical trauma.)

"I had learning problems in school."

Kids who struggle in school commonly experience a nightmare of anxiety, humiliation, and teasing in the classroom and on the playground. If, as an adult, you procrastinate about reading or deskwork, feel anxious in new situations, or are very sensitive to correction or criticism, you may have had a hard time in school.

- *Perfectionist:* I attempted to avoid criticism or disapproval by doing things perfectly.
- *Hero:* I accomplished great things so my parents would be proud of me.
- *Confronter:* I was passionate about the truth no matter the consequences.
- *Scapegoat:* I took the blame for everything and everyone.
- *Surrogate Parent:* I had to take care of situations that were beyond my ability to manage well.
- *Surrogate Spouse:* I had to be there for one of my parents in his/her spouse's absence.
- *Black Sheep:* I was labeled the bad kid for acting out and doing my own thing.

As kids, we initially fill these roles to help our families function more smoothly. But they eventually stifle our development, requiring us to give up important aspects of our personalities and temperaments. Playing a role may mean having to relinquish significant aspects of who God created us to be. Furthermore, when we reach adulthood, these roles often continue to operate, stagnating our emotional and even spiritual growth.

5. If you played one of these roles when you were growing up, identify which one(s) and explain what need it may have met in your family. What did that role do for you? How did it increase or decrease your anxiety?

6. What evidence that you still play this role in adult relationships do you see in your life, if any? In what ways does this role hinder intimacy in your relationships now? Be specific. What do you think would happen in these relationships if you stopped playing this role?

7. Be teachable and ask your spouse for his or her sense of what roles you play in relationships with others. Write down the answer. How does playing each role make you feel? How might you feel if you stopped?

8. Share with your spouse or group members which point was most beneficial to you as you worked through chapter 3.

Ideal Love Lessons: The Secure Connector

A few of us were blessed to have had parents who were attentive and in tune with us as we were growing up, and the result was a generally secure imprint. In chapter 4 of *How We Love,* we looked at the hallmarks of this imprint and its implications for adult relationships. We also discussed the comfort circle and how trust and respect develop in relationships between parents and their children. This chapter of the workbook will prompt you to give more thought to these ideas.

TRUST AND RESPECT

Trust is an essential part of a healthy emotional connection. When we develop the ability to trust from our early days, we become comfortable needing others, and we expect relationships to bring relief and comfort. Of course, this trust can be broken if we are betrayed, badly hurt, or abandoned.

1. Think about your reactions to the word *trust.* Describe those reactions. Then, on a scale from 1 to 10, evaluate how easy it is for you to trust people. What in your past has made it easy or difficult—or somewhere in between—to trust?

2. Do you have difficulty trusting people today? What childhood event(s) involving a family member or someone else taught you that not everyone—or anyone—is trustworthy?

3. Evaluate the level of trust in your marriage. What circumstances, situations, or even people seem to consistently erode that trust? What can you do to stand strong against those forces?

4. What specific actions or choices might increase your ability to trust your spouse?

If we learned to feel and deal—to successfully manage a wide range of emotions—as we grew up, our parents honored and respected us and our feelings. This is not the kind of respect demanded by an angry parent whose motto is "Do as I say and not as I do." True respect does not develop in that kind of family when everyone is playing by different rules. In fact, respect is an attitude that is best taught by example as opposed to being demanded or commanded.

5. Evaluate the level of respect members of your family had for one another as you were growing up.

6. Evaluate the level of respect in your marriage. Do you respect your mate? Why or why not? What impact do your childhood experiences of respect or its absence have on your relationships, specifically on your ability to respect people?

7. Do you feel that trust and respect have to be earned? Why or why not?

8. What aspects of your spouse would you put in the category of Being Human (you trust that person even when he or she makes mistakes and shows weaknesses). What aspects of your spouse would you put in the category of Must Change (you trust that person only after he or she changes)?

9. What childhood memories have you and your spouse shared with each other? Do you have new levels of understanding, empathy, and compassion for each other? What impact does this have on your ability to trust? Explain.

10. What was God's response when Peter broke Jesus's trust? Read Luke 22:54–62 and John 21:15–23 to get the whole story. What do you think God would do with you if you failed Him? What within you would cause you to have trouble restoring others who have broken your trust?

11. You probably know that God created us in His image, but have you considered that your *feelings* are part of God's creation? God, too, has emotions, so despite what you may have learned in your family growing up, emotions aren't bad. In fact, one reason feelings are so important is that they act as a signal telling us what we need. *If we don't know what we feel, we won't know what we need.* Are you willing to ask God to help you recover any emotions that have been suppressed or remain underdeveloped from your childhood? Take a look at the soul words list. Write the three feelings you most often express. List three feelings you rarely express. Write out a prayer about the emotions you are unable to feel or express.

12. When we have feelings and emotions, we have to learn to deal with them appropriately. Review the story about Susie in chapter 4 of *How We Love,* who was learning to feel and deal. Did your parents help you feel and deal? If so, what did they do? If not, what could they have done to help you develop this skill? What particular emotion, if any, is managing you rather than your managing it? Why do you think you struggle to manage this emotion?

13. Evaluate your level of self-care. What do you do to replenish yourself or fill your gas tank? If you don't know, what steps will you take to find out? What aspects of your marriage are being affected—for good or bad—by your ability or inability to take care of yourself? Be specific.

14. Were you able to truly be a child in your home growing up? Explain your answer and support it with evidence from your childhood. Did you have to manage the emotions of one or both of your parents? If so, which emotion(s), and what role did that management lead you to assume?

15. What hallmarks of a secure love style do you feel you lack? (See the list on pages 48–49 of *How We Love.*)

16. What hallmarks of a secure love style do you possess? Does your spouse agree? If you have children, would they agree? If you aren't sure, ask them. (In doing so, you will foster an open atmosphere for growth in your home, and they will love you for it.)

17. Have you known people who seem to stay the same, people who have never changed or grown out of childhood defenses or roles? Why do you think they have remained stuck all their lives?

18. What behavioral change(s) do you see in yourself as you look back over the past year? Be specific. Ask those closest to you what growth and change they have observed in you. If you can't identify any areas, ask those closest to you what they would like to see changed in your life in the upcoming year.

SECURE-CONNECTOR ASSESSMENT

Below is a list of assessment statements that describes a secure connector. Put a check mark by any statement that describes you most of the time as you relate to your spouse. Then record your score on the next page.

_____ I have a wide range of emotions and express them appropriately.

_____ It is easy for me to ask for help and receive from others when I have needs.

_____ I enjoy time with my spouse and also have friends and interests outside my marriage.

_____ I can say no to others even when I know it will upset them.

_____ I will initiate a difficult conversation in order to resolve a problem.

_____ When I want something, I can plan and wait in order to have it.

_____ When I make a mistake, I can recover easily and try again.

_____ I know when I'm wrong and I take responsibility for my actions or attitudes and apologize.

_____ I'm a hard worker and take my responsibilities seriously.

_____ I'm adventuresome and know how to play and have fun.

_____ I know I'm not perfect, and I give my spouse (and kids) room to have weaknesses.

_____ I am able to negotiate and offer compromises when my spouse and I disagree.

_____ I enjoy touch and am affectionate with my family.

_____ I give respect to each member of my family even when they annoy me.

_____ I'm comfortable with emotions and can offer comfort when someone is upset.

Score _____

(Ask your spouse if he or she agrees with your answers.)

19. Take time to discuss your responses with your spouse or group before moving to the next chapter.

Secure connectors believe they are worthy of comfort and that other people are capable of providing relief when asked. To arrive into adulthood with this love style is a rare privilege. In contrast to the other love styles, because of the healthiness that your parents promoted in you, giving and receiving love will be easier for you, and you will find better support during life's difficult moments.

Yet remember that being a secure connector does not mean you are sinless or that you will be completely free from anxiety or conflict. For as the Bible teaches us, simply living in the world means we will be subjected to agitation and angst.

Now we'll move on to exploring some specifics about the five love styles. Even if you feel you've already identified your style and your spouse's style, we recommend you begin by evaluating the assessment statements at the beginning of each chapter and tallying both your scores. If you haven't yet identified your style, try to choose the one or two styles you most strongly identify with and begin working through those chapters. Let's get started.

Part

2

Styles That Impair
How We Love

Chapter 5

The Avoider Love Style

If you are working through this material in a group, we suggest one or two weeks for members to identify their love styles and to share what aspects of themselves placed them in that category. In subsequent weeks, members can then share responses to the questions within the chapter that most describes them. Allow members to go at their own pace and work on different questions as they go. All will benefit from hearing questions raised and challenges faced. Group feedback will be especially useful to those members still attempting to identify their particular styles.

And remember, these questions *cannot* be completed in a week. The goal of this workbook is to promote deep and lasting growth, and that takes time and effort. Uncovering the roots of your present difficulties can take many weeks, even months, but keep at it. If you feel resistant, that's often a sign that you're close. Be patient and allow yourself time to explore. Act on the suggestions for as long as it takes to see results. However, if an issue doesn't seem to apply to you, don't spend time there. Move on and try something else. Keep taking steps forward and allow yourself the necessary time to make healthy changes in how you love.

Most people imprinted to be avoiders make statements like the ones below. Even if you do not think this is your style, read the list and put a check mark by any statement you feel is often true for you. Tally your points at the bottom of the list.

AVOIDER ASSESSMENT

_____ It seems as if my spouse has a lot more emotional needs than I do.

_____ Events, remarks, and interactions with people that are upsetting to my
spouse seem like no big deal to me.

_____ I don't have many memories from my childhood.

_____ I would describe myself as an independent, self-reliant person.

_____ I would rather do something alone than have a long conversation with
someone.

_____ My spouse complains that I don't show enough affection.

_____ When something bad happens, I get over it and move on.

_____ I need my space in relationships and feel annoyed if someone wants
to be with me a lot.

_____ I like to make decisions on my own.

_____ I feel uncomfortable when someone is very emotional, especially if I think
I am supposed to help that person.

_____ In my family growing up, we all sort of did our own thing.

_____ I have siblings with whom I have little to no contact today.

_____ I have never felt particularly close to my parents.

_____ Nothing gets me too bothered or upset.

_____ I rarely cry.

Score _____

(Ask your spouse if he or she agrees with your answers.)

If you are imprinted to be an avoider, this chapter of the workbook is designed to help you grow. We also include a section for those in relationship with a person who has an avoider love style.

1. Read Psalm 69. Make a list of all the feelings described in this song. Circle any of the feelings that you have experienced in the last month.

2. Many times painful events prompt an individual to enter therapy. In fact, over the years, we have recognized that one way God uses painful circumstances in the lives of those imprinted to avoid is to bring their feelings back to the surface again. It is as though God is thawing feelings that were locked away long ago. We sometimes say to such clients or friends, "Perhaps God is using this upsetting event to give you back the feelings you rarely expressed as a child." What event in your life has God used or is currently using to give you back your feelings? Why is this an important gift to you? Consider, for instance, that we are to love God with all our hearts. Can you do that if you've had to deaden your heart to feelings?

One of the most important growth goals for those imprinted to be avoiders is to learn to recognize what you are feeling and to expand your range of emotions. This skill is extremely important, because emotions are linked to needs, and—as we said earlier—if you don't know what you feel, you can't know what you need. We suggest posting the soul words list in a prominent place at home (taped to the remote control?). Also place a copy in your purse or wallet. As you encounter daily events, refer to the list and choose a word that might fit what you are feeling.

3. Looking at the list of soul words at the back of this book, which feelings are the hardest for you to experience or express? Which feelings, if any, do you find more accessible?

4. Reflect on the last time you cried. How old were you? Why did you cry? When, if ever, would tears have been appropriate but you found yourself unable to cry?

5. What happened—or may have happened—in your family growing up that caused you to stop feeling sadness? Journal and/or share with your spouse or group.

6. Do you have memories of being comforted as a child or adult? Share one or two. If you don't have such memories, what do you envision when you imagine someone offering you comfort? Journal and/or share these thoughts.

7. Remember Jack from chapter 5 of *How We Love*? He had few memories of childhood events. In what ways, if any, do you relate to his experience? Talk about your childhood memories—or lack of them—with someone. If no listener is available, journal either some

key memories or specific characteristics of your parents that might explain your avoider love style. Do you remember experiencing emotions during those key memories you recalled? If so, what were they? If you don't remember any emotions, use the soul words list and write down any feelings that would be likely to occur in such circumstances.

Being able to express your childhood memories is important. So seek an opportunity to share your journaling with your spouse. If memories are few, ask siblings or relatives for their memories of you as a child. Even just one sentence from a person who knew you well can help you make sense of your feelings and responses as an adult. Looking at old family pictures may also spur memories.

Besides being unaware of their emotions, individuals with an imprint to avoid are often unaware of sensations in their bodies. So learn to become aware of how your body tenses when you encounter emotions. A tight chest, a clenched jaw, a constricted throat, crossed arms, concave shoulders, and especially constricted breathing are bodily responses we often see in our offices. You may also be unaware of smiling as you describe painful events, and that is a common defense to block pain. All these bodily responses operate outside of our conscious awareness. Noticing and reversing them will help allow emotions to surface. Ask your spouse or group members to tell you when they notice any bodily responses that you may not notice yourself. Their reflections and observations will help you learn about yourself, especially during the sharing of emotions. Your spouse or group members will begin to do for you as an adult what your family was unable to do when you were a child.

8. Are you up for a challenge? Make extended eye contact with your spouse or a group member. Try to lock gazes for one or two minutes. Notice the sensations in your body. What do you experience?

9. Close your eyes and try to imagine your mother's eyes. If they could talk, what would they say to you? Notice your bodily sensations as you do this. Jot down your thoughts and feelings or share your experience with someone you trust. Do the same with your father's eyes. Again, jot down your thoughts and feelings or share your experience with someone you trust.

If you want to be a better listener, especially when you're dealing with another person's difficult emotions or strong feelings, it's important for you to learn not to mentally detach and emotionally disengage. Be courageous. Move toward others when they are upset rather than becoming angry or withdrawing. The first feeling you encounter will probably be anxiety. Expect this—and be encouraged that at least you are feeling! Admit to the person you're with that you are anxious and do not know what to do but that you *will try* to help.

Ask the person if he wishes to vent or problem solve. If he needs to vent, simply say out loud what you observe. For example, "I see this makes you very upset" or "I see you are very mad about what the kids did." Saying what you see is not hard. If the person wishes to problem solve, ask what part of the problem he most needs help with. Offer to brainstorm possible solutions.

Keep a record of your attempts to stay engaged with others when they are emotional. Jot down the subject of the conservation and the date. If you are in a group setting, practice with members of the group. Remember that you are trying to learn a skill you didn't have the opportunity to develop as a young person. Be patient with yourself.

10. Attempt to listen to the feelings of others, then jot down details about what you experienced, including your emotions.

Another valuable exercise is to ask someone for help even if you don't think you need it. Focus on your emotional needs rather than on tasks and jobs. Notice when you feel stressed and ask for something by starting with, "I need…" For example, "I need to talk," "I need a hug," "I need to take a walk with you," or "I need some time alone with you." This will be difficult, so ask God to help you first recognize and then acknowledge your needs. This skill is crucial to growth. Make it your goal to share your needs at least once a day.

11. Write a brief summary of your efforts and feelings as you do this exercise.

12. Learning to include others in your thought and decision-making process is also crucial for closeness. Consult with another person, ideally your spouse, before you make a decision. Ask them for input before you finalize your plans. (Remember, people who are married to avoiders usually feel like they're in the dark.) Summarize your attempts here.

HELPING AVOIDERS

The following suggestions are not meant as a personal guide for how to reform the avoiders in your life. Instead, they are intended to help you better understand and connect with them. You must keep in mind that an injury has prompted their behavior, so have compassion for their struggles and fears about intimacy. Realize, too, that because they have such difficulty with appearing vulnerable, their struggle will not be visible on the surface. So take these suggestions slowly, one at a time. If you try to do everything in one week, you will overwhelm the avoider. Ask God to guide you as you make an effort to support anyone in your life who has the avoider imprint.

13. Before we get to the tips, list people in your life whom you suspect were imprinted to be avoiders. Then write a prayer below asking God to give you more love and understanding for these individuals.

14. Describe a time when you felt angry with one of the people you just listed. What happened? What avoider behavior, if any, prompted or fueled your anger?

Next time you attempt to relationally connect with an avoider, try the following approaches.

Stay calm. Anger repels them and causes them to clam up, as do other intense agitated emotions. If you do get angry, try to express the hurt under your anger. Hopefully, avoiders will be less defensive then. Also, use a low tone of voice and wait patiently for a response. Keep in mind that past injuries have caused this pattern of avoiding, which they do with everyone. So, as much as possible, try not to take their behavior personally. Ask them if there is anything you can do to make it safer for them to open up. Remember, avoiders are awkward when it comes to feeling and communicating emotions. Since they never had opportunities as a child to describe or share their inner feelings and responses, this is new for them. Anger and impatience will send them crawling back into their caves. Wait after you ask a question; let them search for words. If a long time passes, say patiently and warmly, "I'm going to wait until you can put words to your feelings and thoughts. I want to understand."

Give them gentle feedback when they pull away. When the avoiders in your life detach, they may not even be aware of it. You might say, for example, "You seem very detached this evening" or "Could you try to share some part of your day that was stressful for you?" Keep a record of your attempts to draw out the avoider. Notice what works as well as what does not.

Tell them you want to understand their history. When the time seems right, ask them to describe memories of being alone, ignored, or unseen. Help them link feelings to the childhood events they describe (the soul words list can be very helpful). Also invite these avoiders to explore emotions of anger or sadness that could not be expressed in earlier years. Again, ask a question about their feelings and wait. It may take time for them to formulate their thoughts.

Don't discount small efforts. Avoiders often link feelings and needs to shame. As they slowly thaw from their detached state, they will feel very vulnerable, embarrassed, and uncomfortable. Compliment their efforts even if the steps seem insignificant to you. Write down the efforts you have noticed even if they are small. Also, in the space that follows, note the avoider's response to your praise and encouragement. Pray and ask God to help you be aware and ready to take advantage of opportunities for showing your appreciation for the avoider's efforts to connect.

If possible, help avoiders discover their wants and desires as well as interests or talents that were never acknowledged or developed. Avoiders often don't know what they want or desire, what they're interested in or good at, because they were rarely asked about such things when they were growing up. For example, after noting how visually oriented and observant one client was, I encouraged her to purchase some art supplies and express her emerging feelings with color, shapes, and textures. Her talent was incredible, and it came as a total surprise to her. She was reluctant to bring her drawings and paintings into my office to show me, but she did. Then she was bewildered by my true enjoyment and enthusiasm for her work. She had never experienced anyone being so interested in her or her talents.

Extend comfort through words and touch to the avoiders you are close to. Be aware, however, that avoiders (also known as detachers) will be uncomfortable and have trouble accepting tenderness. So expect an awkward response to your efforts, but keep trying. You might say something like, "You look upset and you probably want to be left alone, but come sit by me on the couch and let me put my arm around you." Be playful when possible: "Come here, honey. Even Superman needed Lois Lane." If the avoider is a male, make it clear that this isn't a sexual gesture but that you are offering nonsexual touch and nurture. Keep the two separate, because avoiders often believe that sex and physical intimacy are one and the same.

15. Write about your efforts to approach the avoider(s) in your life as outlined in the previous paragraphs. Make sure to describe the outcome.

Chapter 6

The Pleaser Love Style

Let's look at some statements that are often true for people imprinted to be pleasers. Even if you do not think this is your style, read the list below and put a check mark by any statement you feel is true for you *most of the time*. After you finish, tally your points.

PLEASER ASSESSMENT

_____ I am usually the giver in relationships.

_____ I am good at keeping the peace.

_____ I find I am able to anticipate the needs of my spouse and meet them.

_____ Sometimes I am dishonest in order to avoid conflict.

_____ I am afraid of making my spouse upset or angry.

_____ When there is conflict, I'll give in just to get it over with.

_____ I don't like to be alone.

_____ It really upsets me when I feel someone is mad at me.

_____ When someone requests my help, I have trouble saying no, so I sometimes find myself overcommitted and stressed.

_____ I had a very critical and/or angry parent, and I tried very hard to win his or her approval.

_____ Sometimes I get mad, but I usually don't show it.

_____ I had a parent who never stood up for himself or herself, but passively accepted poor treatment.

_____ When I sense others are distancing themselves from me, I try harder to win them back.

_____ I am on the cautious side; I definitely wouldn't call myself a risk-taker.

_____ I had an overprotective parent who worried a lot.

Score_____

(Ask your spouse if he or she agrees with your answers.)

Perhaps you identify with the pleaser. If so, we hope you are beginning to understand what may have created your imprint. And although such insight is helpful, nothing about us changes unless we choose to grow and practice new behaviors. This chapter of the workbook is going to help direct you along that path of growth.

First a quick observation. It is always amazing to us how many people with this love style are unaware of the anxiety that drives it. This is probably because they were apprehensive as kids and became so accustomed to this sensation that they no longer recognize it as anxiety. Other people with this pleaser imprint are more aware that they are indeed feeling anxious, but they tend to minimize it with statements like "I'm just stressed" or "I'm just concerned." So one of the first steps of healing, as obvious as this may sound, is to admit that your anxiety is high much of the time. Recognizing that you are anxious and fearful of people's responses is a gradual process and can take some time. After all, you may have lived with this anxious feeling for so many years that you don't see it for what it is.

1. If you relate to the pleaser love style, would you call yourself an anxious person? Why or why not? Ask God to help you be aware of when you are feeling anxious. List some recent times when you have noticed this feeling. Then, using a 1–10 scale, rate your general level of anxiety. What types of situations tend to increase your anxiety? What causes it to go down?

2. As we pointed out in the book, this pleaser imprint commonly occurs either when a child's parent is fearful and overprotective or when a parent is angry and critical. If you think you're probably a pleaser, with which of these two situations did you grow up? What details from your childhood experiences might have contributed to this imprint? We hope you have shared some of your family background with your spouse and/or group to help them better understand you. If you have not, take the time to do so.

3. A person's anxiety can block other feelings, especially sadness or anger. If you are a pleaser, do you remember sharing feelings of sadness or anger with one or both of your parents as you were growing up? If not, why not? If so, what was their response? As an adult, how do you deal with sadness? with anger? Do you hide these emotions or share them. Write about these two feelings in your own life.

4. In what ways do you assume the pleasing role in order to keep others from detaching or being angry with you? Give a few specific examples. Also, in what ways do you give in to others to reduce your own anxiety? Ask God to help you see what motivates your giving. Make some notes about your observations.

5. Constantly being in the giving role can keep you out of touch with your own feelings, because you are focusing on the feelings and needs of others. Use the soul words list and write the feelings you are most often aware of. Which emotions do you rarely feel? Why do you think those feelings are difficult for you to access?

6. Now think about yourself as a receiver. What is your response to a compliment? What is your general response to an offer of help? How often do you ask for something from your spouse? What do your answers to these three questions tell you about your ability to receive or how comfortable you are receiving?

7. An important growth goal for pleasers like you is to learn to tolerate other people being angry with you. What is your response when your spouse is angry in general? is angry with *you*? Do you tend to want to quickly fix the situation? If so, why? What do you think would happen if you just let your spouse be upset?

8. Read Psalm 51:6, Ephesians 4:25, and Colossians 3:9. What instructions and insights into what God values are given in these verses? Now read John 8:44 which explains why honesty is so important. Are you ever dishonest in order to avoid conflict? In what areas of your relationship with your spouse do you most struggle to be honest? Practice

initiating honest conversations when you are upset or annoyed with someone rather than avoiding that conflict altogether. Each time make a note of your efforts. What happened, and what was happening inside you?

9. Now read Ephesians 4:26. What is this verse saying to you personally? What can you do to show your anger without sinning?

10. No one likes rejection, but pleasers tend to avoid it at all costs. Most of the time, speaking truth involves a cost—people experience discomfort. Read Luke 4:14–30 and John 6:53–66 and list some examples of the rejection Jesus experienced. In what ways might your behavior be different if you were able to face someone's anger or rebuff?

11. Being alone is sometimes hard for pleasers. Is it hard for you? Why do you think that is? What feelings do you tend to have when you're alone? Were there times you were alone as a child? What happened? Next time you're alone, get the soul words list and see if you can identify how exactly being alone makes you feel. Write about that experience.

12. Pay attention to your breathing. Tense, tight muscles that lead to shallow breathing increase anxiety. You can, however, teach yourself to relax and breathe deeply. The first

step is to notice what is happening with your body. (Shallow breathing, for instance, does not make your belly move.) Take several minutes right now to do so. Relax your forehead; make sure it's nice and smooth. No furrows allowed! Then relax your eyes and jaw. Soften your tongue all the way down your throat. Take a deep, slow breath. As you exhale, let your head drop forward and relax your neck and shoulders. Take five more slow breaths, letting each one move deeper into your belly. Now, as you sit in this relaxed position, pick a simple comforting word or verse and repeat it slowly several times. (If you begin to drool, you're definitely relaxed!) Wasn't that nice? Be good to yourself and do this five or six times a day. It only takes a minute or a minute and a half. Write what you noticed as you started this exercise and how you felt at the end.

13. When your spouse asks for space, time alone, or time with friends, how do you feel? Why do you think you feel that way? Also, do you tend to make your spouse feel guilty if he or she wants some time apart? If so, what exactly do you do and/or say? What impact do your words and actions have on your marriage?

14. Do you enjoy spending some time apart from your spouse? If so, what do you like to do, and why does it help your relationship? If you don't like to be away from your spouse, why do you think that is? What personal interests, hobbies, or activities—if any—do you enjoy that do not include your mate? If you don't have any, why is that? Write one thing you might enjoy if you gave yourself the opportunity to develop outside interests.

15. If you came from a home where you were overprotected, you may feel afraid to try new things. But we encourage you to take a risk and step out of your comfort zone. Think of something you would normally avoid doing and make specific plans to try it. It could be anything. The goal of this exercise is for you to get a taste of not letting fear hold you back from living life. Write what you will try. After you have taken this bold step, share with your spouse or group how the experience was for you.

16. Are decisions usually difficult for you? What types of decisions do you most often avoid? Make a decision—not necessarily a big one—on your own without asking anyone for permission, advice, or reassurance. Flexing your muscles of independence in small ways like this will build your confidence. Write about your experience.

17. Do you have difficulty saying no when others request your time, attention, or help? Do you struggle with being overly committed? Do you feel that others take advantage of your generous nature? Perhaps you need to limit your giving by learning to say no. Write a simple, straightforward sentence expressing a limit (for example, "I can't help; my schedule is full.") and practice saying it out loud so you can hear yourself say the words. Write about when you actually use your sentence in a real situation. Remember, people are used to your always saying yes. Prepare yourself for a look of surprise or even some objection when you say no.

18. When pleasers want to control something, their goal is usually to keep their world predictable and safe. Carefully planning ahead and knowing what to expect can also lower their anxiety. In what areas of life do you see yourself being controlling in order to lower your anxiety?

19. Are you direct or indirect when you communicate? Why? And how does your spouse react?

20. People are generally more patient when they can see that you are making an obvious effort to grow. But being a bit more adventuresome and spontaneous may bring you face to face with your anxiety. Knowing that your effort will be worth it, write one specific thing you are willing to do that you have been reluctant to do. Plan ahead of time how you can best be supported. What will help you more—words of reassurance and encouragement, holding someone's hand, a hug, reminders to breathe, or something else?

Sometimes, in spite of your best efforts, your anxiety might continue to be overwhelming. If that's the case, don't suffer needlessly. Seek help from a medical doctor, preferably a psychiatrist who can prescribe medications that can recalibrate your brain chemistry. Some drugs that help with anxiety can be addictive, but many are not. Actually, drug and alcohol abuse are often people's attempts to self-medicate their anxiety. Let us reassure you that we have seen many, many lives transformed by the proper use of medication.

HELPING PLEASERS

Keep in mind that the primary difficult emotion for pleasers is anxiety. When they are pushed too far past their comfort zone, you will notice a reaction of some kind, and it will likely be anxiety based. Maybe your spouse has never identified his or her inner experience as anxiety. If this is true, the soul words list can be helpful during any discussion. It is especially hard for men to admit they feel anxious, scared, or insecure. It may take some encouragement and acceptance for them to open up and begin to have words for what is in their hearts. If your spouse can't identify his or her anxiety but you suspect it's there, write a prayer asking God to reveal this. Remember, God is usually more gentle and patient than we might be, so be willing to wait for an answer.

Develop compassion for the pleaser's anxiety by understanding the childhood experiences that contributed to this problem. Take time to ask about family memories and about the times they were scared, traumatized, teased, or overprotected. You may also need to explore the possibility of an overly critical or angry parent and the impact of that relationship in creating fear and anxiety. Finally, remember the question at the beginning of the workbook about what annoys you most in your spouse? One of my biggest complaints about Milan was that he was always asking me, "How are you?" After listening to him talk about his childhood memories, though, I understood why he felt so compelled to need to know my mood. My irritation was greatly reduced, and for the first time I began to feel compassion for his struggle. In light of my experience, I encourage you to make a note of what you learn about your spouse. Review those lessons when you find yourself feeling annoyed with him or her.

After pleasers have identified some of their childhood memories, *encourage them to explore feelings, such as sadness and anger, that may underlie their anxiety.* Also, regularly ask them directly how they are coping: "How is your anxiety level today?" Offer to hold and comfort pleasers as they become aware of the impact of the early years in creating an imprint of insecurity and fear. A man will sometimes be willing to stretch out on the couch and put his head in his wife's lap. This position communicates to a man, "You are the focus of my time and attention, and I'm here to listen and care for you." At times you may begin to feel sympathy. Express those feelings and any others. Seeing your feelings can help pleasers pull their own feelings toward the surface.

When pleasers make an effort to face their fears, offer acceptance and reassurance. Tell them you will patiently support their efforts to overcome their worries. Your doing so shows them that you are not overwhelmed by their feelings, and it provides them with *containment,* a newfound sense of stability and safety, which will become a basis for their newly emerging security base.

Encourage pleasers to stretch beyond their comfort level. Develop a plan, for instance, that gradually promotes separation from you in amounts that are increasingly tolerable. Also engage with pleasers in new activities that will help them learn to be comfortable in the areas they fear. You will be helping them discover as adults what they missed as children—that they can conquer fear instead of giving in to it. Be patient and encouraging, yet firm. Pray for wisdom about when to push and when to be compassionate and tolerant.

21. Write about your efforts to approach the pleaser(s) in your life as outlined in the previous paragraphs. Make sure to describe the outcome.

Chapter 7

The Vacillator Love Style

Vacillators may identify with many of the statements below. But even if you don't think this is your style, read through the list and put a check mark next to any statements that remind you of yourself. Tally your points at the bottom of the list.

VACILLATOR ASSESSMENT

_____ I feel like no one has ever really understood what I need.

_____ I was instantly attracted to my spouse, and our early relationship was intense and passionate.

_____ I hope for more in my relationships than I get; I am often disappointed as time goes on.

_____ When my spouse tries to respond to my needs, I feel it is too little too late.

_____ I am a very passionate person and feel things deeply.

_____ I could list many times my spouse has hurt and disappointed me.

_____ I can really sense when others pull away from me.

_____ I want far more connection with my spouse than I have.

_____ I like the feeling of making up after a fight.

_____ When people hurt me long enough, I write them off.

_____ If my spouse would pursue me more often and more passionately, our relationship would be better.

_____ I don't like to be alone, but when my spouse is around, I feel angry and empty.

_____ My parent(s) still drive me crazy.

_____ Sometimes I find myself picking fights, and I'm really not sure why.

_____ I make it obvious when I'm hurt, and when my spouse does not pursue me and ask what's wrong, I hurt more.

_____ It seems I end up waiting for my spouse to be available and pay attention to me.

Score_____

(Ask your spouse if he or she agrees with your answers.)

The vacillator imprint is formed when a child is raised in a home where there is some connection and bonding, but it is sporadic, unpredictable, and governed by the mood of the parent rather than the needs of the child. Left in a constant state of wanting and waiting, vacillators grow up looking for consistent attention, yet they cannot trust others to truly provide it. They idealize new relationships and then feel angry and hurt when their high expectations are not met. They create a push-pull (I want you/I don't want you) feeling within relationships. They can feel madly in love one minute and then deeply hurt and hateful the next.

1. What parts of chapter 7 in *How We Love* did you relate to? What circumstances in your home growing up contributed to your vacillator imprint? Do you remember hoping and waiting for connection or attention? Describe one or two of those times. Did you experience abandonment? Explain the situation and note how old you were. Was one of your parents inconsistent or unpredictable? If so, describe how. List some disappointments you experienced during your growing-up years. Write down some key memories and the feelings that characterized those memories. Share these memories and feelings with your spouse or small group.

2. After contemplating the feelings prompted by the memories above, consider how often you experience these same feelings with your spouse. Write down any similarities between past feelings and present feelings.

3. Do you remember feeling sad or angry as a child? If so, what brought on the sadness? the anger? What did you do with these feelings, and what were your parents' reactions?

4. It is very important for you to both develop self-reflection skills and come to understand the origins of your imprint. After all, your expectations for relationships, as well as your reactions to people disappointing you, are fed by your childhood wounds. You must therefore acknowledge and accept that you probably have a strong desire to find a person who can relieve all your "bad" feelings by being close, staying engaged, and giving you lots of attention. The agitation and uncertainty you feel when this does not happen isn't new. You felt it countless times as a child. So continue to review childhood memories and ask God to help you identify the roots of your imprint. This exercise means taking the focus off your current relationships and everything people do to hurt or anger you. Instead, spend a season looking inward and asking God to reveal the wounds that drive your current feelings, behaviors, and reactions. That truth will begin to set you free. Write down the insights God brings you as you continue to pray this prayer.

5. More than people with any other love style, vacillators tend to idealize romance. They enjoy the intense early phases of a relationship when each partner is paying a lot of attention to the other. It can therefore be difficult for vacillators to make the transition to real life. They feel as though all the passion has gone out of the relationship, and it is harder to sense that excitement and love. As disappointment sets in, so does anger, and the vacillator may put pressure on the spouse to rekindle those original feelings, because the feelings of loss trigger painful memories. Has this dynamic occurred in your marriage or in other relationships? Describe.

6. Experiencing healing means you must recognize the ways your love style drives you to find the magical person who will make you consistently feel special and wanted so you will never again have to feel anxious about rejection or abandonment. Right now, though, list the important people in your life whom you are currently idealizing. Among those people may be a friend, pastor, boyfriend or girlfriend, or therapist, but you will most likely notice that you're listing fairly new relationships. Next, make yourself write three of each of these people's weaknesses and human limitations. Ask yourself why you need to see them as so wonderful and "all good." What do you feel when you see in black and white the faults and weaknesses of the people on your list?

7. You will have a tendency to devalue your long-term relationships and see little good in those people who have disappointed you. So right now list those people who have hurt you or let you down. Next to each person's name list three positive qualities. Make a

point of telling those people what you appreciate about them. You may feel that you already do this, but tell them anyway.

8. Read Romans 12:9–21 and Hebrews 12:14–15. What is God saying to you through these scriptures about your relationships, present or past? What action steps is He prompting you to take? What could you do to make obedience to these verses more a part of your life? Be very specific. By the way, even if it is best for you to have no contact with someone, have you forgiven that person for hurting you? Explain your answer.

9. Write down some things you are currently angry about in your marriage. Then get out the soul words list and try to determine which emotions underlie your anger. Too often vacillators use vague words like *bad, yucky,* or *awful,* but those words don't readily identify a specific feeling. So, again, look at your list of things you are angry about and write down the specific feelings that are submerged under the anger.

10. When you feel angry in the future, remind yourself to identify what feeling is underneath the anger, and share that emotion with your spouse. Anger tends to repel others and make them defensive, but other feelings can invite openness and intimacy. So instead of saying, "I'm sick and tired of your promises to be home for dinner. Just don't bother coming home," express your sadness: "I'm sad you aren't coming home for dinner. I was

looking forward to sharing some things about my day and hearing about yours." There are times when anger is appropriate, but it is also helpful to learn to communicate the more vulnerable feelings that underlie the anger. When you do, you have a greater chance of being heard. Write about your experience of communicating your anger differently or, even better, about communicating the feelings underneath that anger.

11. Vacillators have a keen awareness of closeness and distance in relationships. In the first part chapter 7 of *How We Love,* Lea described how she was watching and waiting, hoping her mom would again give her the kind of physical affection she had shown Lea in the hospital. Lea grew very proficient at reading her mom's moods to determine how likely it was that her desire would be fulfilled. In what ways does Lea's experience remind you of yourself? What gauging of other people's moods did you have to do when you were growing up? Write down some of your memories.

When you were a kid, you had to guess about what might happen. You had to completely rely on your own assumptions. So you learned to constantly read between the lines in an attempt to determine what to expect and how to respond. You may not even be aware of how much you still read body language and the moods and actions of others to determine whether you are wanted or unwanted, liked or disliked, accepted or rejected. To you, relationships are a guessing game, and your assumptions may or may not be accurate. In fact, the actions and reactions of others are not always about you at all, but you probably assume they are.

You will never know the truth about people's thoughts or feelings toward you until you learn to check your assumptions by directly asking them about your concerns. If, for instance, you don't feel comfortable in a certain situation, you may conclude that the other person has negative feelings toward you, but that simply may not be the case. So ask! (If the person does have some negative feelings, at least you will know for sure! And now you have a chance to address whatever issue is causing the feelings.)

Your feelings are real, but you may be imagining the other person's intentions or feelings. If you leave these imagined injuries unmanaged and unchecked, you may find yourself depositing them in the bank of bitterness and resentment, and that account accrues interest as you continue to make other deposits. Over time, your level of anger and bitterness will grow. Because those emotions can be so destructive, keeping short accounts and checking assumptions are critical for healthy relationships and personal growth.

12. Identify some recent assumptions you have made about situations or people that you believe are true, but are—now that you think about it—merely guesses. Write them below. Next, share your assumptions with your spouse, friend, or group. How do you feel as you take this step? Ask for a hug if you need it, and don't be afraid to cry.

13. In the week ahead, ask God to help you be aware of your tendency to make assumptions and guesses as you interact with others. Verbally check any assumptions you notice. You might say, for example, "You seem distant. Did I do something to upset you?" or "I can tell you are sad. I need to know if it's about something I did." Make notes about these times when you check your assumptions.

A lot of indirect communication goes on in the childhood home of a vacillator. As Lea grew up, for instance, her mom would be mad at her dad. Her mom communicated her displeasure by leaving the house and spending time only with Lea. In one session Lea said her mom could pout for weeks and sometimes would even ignore Lea. Learn to recognize when you communicate in an indirect manner, and develop the ability to speak more openly and truthfully. In other words, say your feelings and thoughts rather than showing them.

14. In what situations and in what specific ways do you act out your feelings rather than talking about them directly? Write down some examples. Then write a direct statement that clearly communicates your thoughts and feelings. Your spouse isn't a mind reader, so practice saying your feelings rather than showing them. Note the results.

15. During an argument, do you tend to bring up the past? Sometimes vacillators have been flooded with so many hurts throughout the years that, when conflict arises, past pain surfaces and overwhelms the vacillator and then, because of that, the spouse as well. So when you are upset, focus on *one topic* without bringing up every complaint about past behavior. Share something you appreciate about your spouse as well as what has upset you. If at the time you cannot think of anything good about your spouse, realize that you have made that person "all bad" in your mind. Remember, every person, every day, every vacation, every church, every friend, every holiday—you get the idea—is both good *and* bad. Being balanced means we are aware of both the good and the bad at any given moment, even in the middle of an argument. Write the results of your efforts to stick to the topic and to share words of appreciation alongside your complaint.

If your level of reactivity remains high and seems impossible to manage, seek the help of a professional. Extreme mood swings or uncontrollable rage can indicate chemical imbalances in the brain that may be a result of early trauma, medical problems, or genetic predispositions. We have both been amazed at the positive impact proper diagnosis and treatment can have in promoting healing and health.

HELPING VACILLATORS

If you are married to a vacillator, the following suggestions may be helpful. Work on one of these at a time. Also, your spouse would probably appreciate being able to choose which one would mean the most to him or her.

Don't allow the vacillator to pull you into extreme all-or-nothing thinking. Hold to middle ground. Record your experiences of striving for balance.

One of the most common complaints we hear about vacillators is, "They are so reactive." And they are—but *keep in mind that painful childhood experiences are at the root of this reactivity.* Ask your mate questions about childhood experiences and explore how he or she felt at the time. You will probably discover that, under all that anger, is a great deal of unacknowledged anxiety and pain. As children, vacillators were probably unable to think or speak about their own internal experiences when they were upset or distressed. They are, however, often unaware of their early wounds or the absence of comfort in their homes during their formative years. Childhood photographs can be helpful in spurring memories. Note some of the things you discover that help you better understand your spouse.

The antidote for anger is grief. Angry individuals, however, block the more vulnerable emotions of sadness or fear with their anger. During a conflict, the vacillator's anger may turn into tears of total frustration, but those are quite different from tears of unadulterated grief over painful childhood experiences. Pray and ask God to reveal memories that are crucial to understanding current conflicts in your marriage. Sadness and tears are essential to healing. Be tender and comforting as you search for memories attached to your spouse's sadness and grief. Write what you learn from the times you do this.

When your spouse has an angry outburst, here's a way to handle it. Learn the following words for those times when your spouse—or any other vacillator you know—is angry and reactive: "I see how upset you are. I want to listen, and I *will* listen when you can calm down. Then you'll be able to tell me what hurt you before you got so angry." If the anger continues, repeat these statements several more times. If necessary, end the conversation by saying, "I am willing to listen when you are able to share your hurt feelings. Let me know when you are ready." Be faithful to your promise and give positive feedback when the vacillator is willing to make an effort. Afterward explain how much easier it is for you to listen and stay engaged when the tone of voice is soft and vulnerable instead of harsh and insulting. We suggest you stick with this approach even if you don't get good responses initially. Note your experiences.

It is difficult to be honest about your own shortcomings, because vacillators tend to do a lot of blaming. They see you as the problem and rarely admit their own contributions to any difficulties. This behavior can set up a pattern of blame, defense, and escalating anger, but you can break that pattern. *Humble yourself and agree when you know your spouse is making a valid point.* Also, know that times of mutual confession and prayer can be productive and healing. Write about a confession you made and the effect it had on the other person and the argument.

Be aware of the temptation to avoid conflict with vacillators by appeasing them or being dishonest. Some vacillators are married to passive spouses who take the road of least resistance, but that's not helpful or healthy. Instead, speak the truth in love and learn to set limits. Initially, this approach will make vacillators more agitated, but you will earn their respect—and keep your self-respect and dignity—by doing so. Note a time when you spoke the truth in love.

In calmer moments, when the agitation level is low, *gently explain to your spouse the effect of his or her anger and how it makes you feel.* Ask for input for ways you two could communicate in calmer, nonreactive ways. In the case of physical abuse or violence, call 911. Such swift action clearly sends the message that violence will not be tolerated.

As disappointment increases and problems multiply, the vacillator can devalue your marriage relationship and make you feel that you cannot do anything right. (If you lived with a critical parent, this may be a familiar and unsettling feeling for you.) When that happens, *solicit help from others to help you sort out which complaints are valid and to remind you of your positive attributes.* Also learn to directly ask the vacillator for positive feedback: "I'm willing to listen to your complaint, but it would really help me if you acknowledged some positive aspects of our relationship as well." Finally, ask your spouse to join you for coffee or a date with the specific purpose of sharing things you appreciate about each other. Write about how you felt—about yourself, your spouse, your relationship—after that time of appreciation.

16. Write about your efforts to approach the vacillator(s) in your life as outlined in the previous paragraphs. Make sure to describe the outcome.

The Chaotic (Controller and Victim) Love Styles

We learned in chapter 8 of *How We Love* that a chaotic environment produces one of these two chaotic love styles. Relationships in such an environment are rarely safe and nurturing; instead they are destructive and dangerous. Some children respond by internalizing their anger and trying to be invisible; they become imprinted as victims and accept abuse quietly. Other children openly display their anger, especially when they are teenagers, exhibiting the controller imprint. As adults, victims will fearfully allow others to dominate them, while the angry victimizer will intimidate those who are weaker.

This chapter has two sets of statements. Even if you don't think either reflects your style, read through both groups of statements and put a check mark by any statement that is true for you most of the time. Tally your points at the bottom of the list.

Victim Assessment

_____ I grew up in a family with serious problems, such as outbursts of anger, violence, addictions, abuse, and neglect.

_____ I have to keep my mate from knowing certain things, because he or she would be angry.

_____ I have a history of being in or even staying in destructive relationships.

_____ I suffer with depression and/or anxiety, and that makes it hard for me to cope with life.

_____ I am loyal even when I realize others are probably exploiting me.

_____ For most of my life, I have felt unworthy and unlovable.

_____ A lot of the time my mind is far off, and I feel emotionally flat, detached, and disengaged.

_____ My parents had drug and alcohol problems.

_____ One of my parents was abusive and the other passive.

_____ I feel as though I functioned as the parent in my home when I was growing up.

_____ My spouse mistreats me, but I stay because it would be worse to be alone.

_____ I was physically, emotionally, or sexually abused during my childhood—or I saw these things happening to other people.

_____ I get nervous when things are calm because I know it won't last, so I'm always waiting for my spouse to get angry or critical.

_____ Sometimes I feel life isn't worth living.

_____ I don't let myself cry, because if I started, I'd never stop.

Score_____

CONTROLLER ASSESSMENT

_____ Growing up, I had an angry parent or sibling who threatened me, intimidated me, and/or was violent toward me.

_____ No one protected me from harm when I was growing up.

_____ My spouse does things behind my back.

_____ I feel angry when other people try to control me or tell me what to do.

_____ I have problems with alcohol, drugs, pornography, gambling, or overspending.

_____ My life is one problem after another, and that means constant stress.

_____ Sometimes I try to control my temper, but I feel too angry to stop raging.

_____ My spouse does things that make me jealous.

_____ I lose my temper a lot, especially at home, but my spouse (or kid) deserves it.

_____ I have hit or pushed my spouse—or I have come very close to doing so.

_____ I change jobs a lot.

_____ By the time I was a teenager, people knew not to mess with me.

_____ By the time I left home, some family members were afraid of me.

_____ My spouse ignores me when I ask him or her to do things a certain way.

_____ My spouse starts most of our fights, because he or she doesn't listen to what I say.

Score_____

GROWTH GOALS FOR BOTH THE VICTIM AND THE CONTROLLER

The first steps of growth and healing almost always take place outside the home in a counselor's office where victims as well as controllers can experience safety and support for the first time in their lives. (That's why this chapter doesn't include couples' exercises.) We share the following suggestions, however, in hope that they can help get the healing process started.

As we have explained, chaotic homes tend to push individuals to one of two opposite poles, resulting in two very different imprints. First we will look at goals that could benefit both the victim and the controller. Then we will consider separate growth goals for each.

Whether you relate to the imprint of the victim or the controller, you first need to acknowledge that you do have an injured love style. While this sounds simple enough, it is not easy to do. After all, chaos and stress seem normal, because that is the way life has always been. Also complicating your healing journey is the fact that it is almost impossible to heal from these injuries without assistance, but asking for help is probably a foreign concept to you. Nevertheless, you will most likely have to seek outside help—and when you experience that safe, loving environment for the first time ever, you will begin to understand what you have been missing all your life.

But where on earth can you find a safe place? First, pray and ask God to lead you to the best resources for you. Then get on the phone and call churches in your area to find out if they have recovery groups. If so, try one out. You can also look for a Christian-based Twelve Step program. There are groups for kids, teens, and adults—and for just about every problem imaginable. Since addictions are almost a universal problem in chaotic homes, there is a dual benefit to selecting a Twelve Step group that addresses the types of issues with which you struggle. In such a setting, you can address your problems with addictions at the same time that you are learning to build honest, trusting, safe relationships. Additionally, Twelve Step groups provide each participant with a sponsor or mentor who is further down the road of healing and recovery. These groups are free and life changing, so there is no excuse for not seeking help. We have seen clients make amazing progress from getting involved in a support group.

List the churches and groups you can contact in an effort to find help and support.

Once you're in a supportive environment, you can begin to talk about your memories of early abuse and ask others to help you determine their effect on your current functioning as an adult. You need to learn how to identify and express your feelings as well as your needs. This will probably be a new experience, because your feelings have probably never been acknowledged or validated. Also, know that feelings of shame—common for people who have chaotic backgrounds—and humiliation only go away when you share your secrets and experience grace, acceptance, and love.

Counselors, support groups, or mentors will give you other opportunities to learn to receive comfort and compassion as they validate the painful effects of your childhood abuse. You probably have grief tucked deep down inside that had no place to go when you were little. Being able to finally grieve over the parenting, love, and acceptance you didn't receive as a child can be incredibly redemptive and healing. And slowly, over time, a new imprint begins to form in your soul, one that will replace the imprint of chaos, rejection, humiliation, and fear.

Finally, it's no surprise that people from chaotic homes can have serious difficulties in their marriages and relationships. The help that is required goes beyond the scope of this workbook. Our goal is to get you started on the road to healing by helping you acknowledge the problems and encouraging you to ask for the help you need.

Growth for the Victim

The victim imprint is somewhat similar to the pleaser imprint, so you may find some questions in that section of the workbook helpful. But while pleasers are willing to put up with a lot, they draw the line at abuse. The victim, however, does not see the line and tolerates the intolerable.

If you are a victim, the first concern you need to address is that of safety. If you or your children are being abused, you need to find a shelter where all of you can receive safety, support, and counseling. Call and gather information so you have an idea what to expect in terms of the emotions you may feel and the protective steps that are needed to guard you against possible angry and dangerous responses from your spouse. You have probably lived for a while with the hope that things at home will get better. But usually the pattern keeps repeating itself, getting worse, not better. As long as fear keeps you frozen, it is impossible to begin the process of healing.

If fear of reprisal from the angry controller in your life is, in fact, preventing you from taking action, you must acknowledge the seriousness of the situation. Nothing in your marriage or your family life will change until you ask for help. Your tendency to minimize problems in your home and excuse your spouse's behavior keeps you from seeking assistance. Asking for help requires you, first, to realize that the situation is beyond your ability to change without help and then to admit that truth to another person—and God encourages us to speak the truth.

1. In what ways do you minimize the problems in your marriage? Give a few specific examples.

2. List some of the excuses you make for your spouse.

3. What do you do to cover and disguise the truth of what goes on in your home? In what ways, if any, are your public life and your private life different? Again, give a few examples.

4. What does your spouse do that makes you afraid?

5. Do you remember feeling that same way in your home growing up? What were you afraid of then?

6. When you were growing up, did you ever say "No!" or "Stop!" when someone was treating you badly? If so, was it difficult for you to confront them, and what happened? If not, what were you feeling?

7. Do you ever say "No!" or "Stop!" to your spouse? If not, what are you feeling? What do you wish for or ask God to do for you during these moments?

8. When you give in to your spouse's requests/demands, do you respect yourself? Why or why not? Does your spouse respect you? Support your answers with evidence.

Most people imprinted to be victims have difficulty saying no and taking firm action when they are mistreated. You will need to learn to set boundaries and make them stick.

9. What health problems, if any, are you dealing with? What do you think your body is telling you that you are refusing to acknowledge? If your symptoms could speak, what would they say?

Once you have found a safe environment, you will need to grow in your ability to enjoy periods of calm by learning to recognize and soothe your underlying anxiety. Detoxifying your mind and body from the adrenaline, anxiety, and constant stress it's used to will take time. Music, deep breathing, and relaxation exercises may help. Speaking words of comfort to the anxious "child part" inside you can also provide new messages of hope. You might, for instance, say, "It's okay to relax, because I'm learning how to keep you safe."

You may be afraid to get angry with your spouse, but you may find it harder to hold back those impulses with your children or pets. If anger is a problem, know that it won't get better until you get help. One caller to the *New Life Live!* radio show confessed to violently shaking her dog when she was upset, and she was worried about someday doing this to her child. We immediately confirmed that this was a likelihood and that she needed to get outside help to better understand and control her rage.

10. Do you struggle with anger when dealing with your children? Support your answer with specific scenes from your life.

11. If you are surprised by the intensity of the anger your children can spark in you, have you ever admitted this to anyone or attempted to get help? Explain. Do you see your anger as a character flaw or a result of your childhood experiences? Explain what you think the source of your anger is.

Some victims rarely feel angry with anyone, even their children. If this is true for you, we are going to make an educated guess that you probably struggle with depression, that you find it easier to be angry with yourself than with another person. You need to recover the feeling of anger if you were never allowed to express it as a child. Constructive anger, properly displayed, is essential to health and growth. The goal is not to eliminate anger, but to learn how to effectively communicate and deal with it. A display of controlled, productive anger should not set off fear in the people around you (as does a violent rage).

12. Do you struggle to express or even feel anger? Explain.

Have you ever witnessed someone display their anger appropriately? Jesus exhibited appropriate anger by being direct about infractions, adjusting his tone and intensity depending on the maturity level of the person(s), stating the truth that had been violated, not being demeaning, and telling the person(s) not to do it again. Further, Jesus expected people to become agitated and experience conflicted emotions, but He didn't try to protect them from feelings of guilt. He told them He loved them and that their sins grieved His heart. Yet He offered them restoration if they would comply with His request, and He gave them grace and mercy when they repented. When He restored them, He didn't hold a grudge.

13. What elements of Jesus's appropriate display of anger would you have liked to experience more of as a child? What aspects would you like to see more developed in your own behavior as a spouse and/or parent?

Growth for the Controller

Considering the home in which you grew up, anger is an appropriate feeling for you to have. The trouble is, anger is probably the only emotion you feel, and it is probably directed at people in your life today who had absolutely nothing to do with making your life miserable when you were young. So what are you to do with all your anger?

We have only seen one thing really lower the level of anger, and that is having the freedom to grieve. Learning to *grieve* your childhood injuries and losses will give you a greater sense of peace, and the more you grieve, the less angry you will be. We have observed this over and over as we've worked with angry people. Grief and sadness are always blocked in chaotic homes, and anger can become a defense against feeling the hurt, especially for men. Furthermore, any vulnerable emotion is often associated with humiliation, shame, and dread. Reviving feelings of grief—definitely a vulnerable emotion—will take courage, time, and a safe person who is willing to listen.

14. Have you ever considered the idea that your anger blocks sadness and grief? What reasons for sadness and grief did you experience as a child? Why might you have chosen to feel anger rather than sadness?

15. Remember Doug in chapter 8 of *How We Love*? It was hard for him to remember or even guess what his feelings were during all the terrible things that went on in his home when he was a child. In what ways, if any, are you like Doug?

Eventually, as your anger and grief subside, you will be able to forgive the person or people who hurt you—even if they are no longer alive. Forgiveness can be defined as "letting the offender out of jail so that you can go free."

The flip side of forgiveness is beginning to take responsibility for the hurtful things you have said and done, to confess those words and deeds, and to ask forgiveness from those you have hurt. It is amazing how much healing can occur as we begin to confess our own shortcomings and sinful behaviors. Besides, such honesty, vulnerability, and transparency are the key character qualities that allow others to trust us and feel safe around us.

HELPING VICTIMS

If you are in a relationship with a victim, the following suggestions may be helpful.

Our goal is to *recognize that much of the fearful reactivity of victims is fueled by childhood injuries.* Politely request permission to ask them questions about their childhood experiences, exploring how they *felt* during those events. Remind them that they can stop or alter the conversation at any time. Under their fear and anger is a great deal of unacknowledged anxiety and hurt. As children, victims were unable to speak about their internal experiences when distressed. They often don't even recognize their early wounds or the absence of comfort.

One antidote to their fear and anxiety is appropriate anger and grief. People who are frozen in fear often block the more vulnerable emotion of sadness. As an essential component of healing, victims need safe places to learn to grieve the painful childhood experiences and shed tears. Ask God to reveal memories that are crucial to understanding current conflicts. Be tender and comforting as you explore memories attached to their sadness and grief.

Remember that because the *victim's prevailing emotion is fear, they will try to conform to their surroundings.* Invite them to speak their mind freely, assuring them that they are safe—they can express their own opinion and disagree with you. Role play with them (if they are willing), pretending you are a parent or other significant person who may have harmed them. Reassure them about their safety as needed.

Because victims have experienced a very disorganized environment growing up, *they will struggle to pull their thoughts together and formulate their words.* Give them time to answer, and don't put words in their mouth. Smile, use soft tones, let them know you understand this is difficult, and tell them to take their time. Treat them with complete respect.

Victims struggle with assertiveness and lack boundaries. Encourage them to set boundaries and learn to say no to demands and requests. Invite them to practice saying no aloud, and help them find and set areas of emotional safety. Let them know they can say no to you without harming the relationship.

Individuals with the victim love style have rarely had anyone acknowledge their positive attributes. They are in desperate need of praise and encouragement, even though they may have a hard time believing it. Let them know you believe in them and reinforce that they have worth and value. By doing so, you will help them experience a healthy new self-image. Be patient, as healing will take time.

HELPING CONTROLLERS

If you are in a relationship with a controller, the following suggestions may be helpful. Again, your safety is extremely important. So before attempting any of these suggestions, determine—

with the help of your support system—both the safety of trying any intervention and the wisest timing for doing so.

Our goal is to *recognize that much of the reactivity of controllers is fueled by childhood injuries.* If you feel it is safe doing so, ask questions about their early experiences and, as they share memories, explore how they felt during those childhood events. Under all their anger is a great deal of unacknowledged anxiety and hurt. When they were children, people with this love style were unable to speak about their own internal experiences when they were upset and distressed. They often don't recognize their early wounds or the absence of comfort in their homes during their formative years.

Again, *the antidote to anger is grief.* Angry individuals block the more vulnerable emotions of sadness or fear with anger. Controllers need to learn to shed tears and grieve over their painful childhood experiences. The emergence of sadness and tears is essential to healing. So pray and ask God to reveal memories that are crucial to understanding current conflicts. Then be tender and comforting as you explore memories attached to their sadness and grief.

The most intense, unproductive fights often occur between partners with chaotic love styles. If you are married to a controller, you can change the dynamic by *refusing to talk until there is no yelling or insulting.* Learn the following mantra and repeat it often when anger erupts. Calmly make eye contact, and in a soft, caring voice say, "I see how upset you are. I want to listen. But it will be easier for me to listen if you stop yelling." If the yelling continues, end the conversation by saying, "I am willing to listen when you can stop yelling. Let me know when you're ready." Be faithful to your promise: listen when the yelling stops. Also, give positive feedback when the controlling individual makes an effort in this area. Explain how much easier it is for you to listen and stay engaged when the tone of voice is soft and vulnerable instead of harsh and insulting. As we do in our offices, be willing to talk about your own love-style injury and the fact that all of us are wounded. Your humble confession will allow the shame, so prevalent in controllers, to be less intense. Such mutual times of confession can be productive and healing.

Be aware of the temptation to avoid conflict with controllers by appeasing them, trying to fix them, or being dishonest. Many of us are used to taking the road of least resistance, but that's not helpful or healthy. Instead, speak the truth in love and learn to set limits. Initially this approach can make controllers more agitated, but by doing so, you will earn their respect—and maintain your self-respect and dignity. Also, keep yourself safe. Taking yourself and your children to a safe place is a way of communicating limits. In the case of physical abuse or violence, call 911. Such swift action clearly sends the message that violence will not be tolerated.

Controllers have rarely had anyone acknowledge any positive aspect of their personhood. They are in desperate need of praise and positive words, even though they may have a hard time believing them. So persevere. Let those wounded adults know—again and again—why you love them.

Chapter 9

Identifying Your Love Style

1. Now that you have read detailed descriptions of each imprint, note below the imprint(s) that most accurately describe you. (You may see yourself as a combination of styles.) List the main beliefs and behaviors in your life that make you identify with the particular style(s). If you see yourself as a combination, which style causes the most problems in your marriage?

2. Which imprint best fits your spouse? List the behaviors and beliefs that caused you to choose that particular imprint for him or her. If you see your spouse as a combination, which style do you think causes the most problems in your marriage?

3. Do you and your spouse agree about which imprint best describes each of you? If not, which close friends could share their observations?

4. In what ways do you identify with the core of anxiety that lies at the heart of each of these love styles? At what point in your childhood can you first pinpoint that feeling of anxiety?

Now take a moment to consider the common lies each love style believes:
- *Avoider:* I don't need anyone.
- *Pleaser:* I am responsible to maintain the happiness and well-being of others, because conflict and rejection are deadly and to be avoided at all costs.
- *Vacillator:* My spouse is the problem in my marriage. There is nothing I can do to improve my marriage because my husband/wife won't change. I need my spouse to take away my bad feelings.
- *Controller:* I have to control and intimidate in order to get what I want.
- *Victim:* If I tried harder in my relationship, my spouse wouldn't get so angry.

5. As you come to better understand your imprint, you may be able to identify other distortions of the truth. For now, see if you can write a corresponding statement of truth for each of the lies (for all five love styles).

Avoider

Pleaser

Vacillator

Controller

Victim

6. In the Bible, Satan is described as the "father of lies" (John 8:44). When God reveals a truth to us, we have an opportunity to recognize it and take control of our thought processes (see 2 Corinthians 10:3–6). Why does believing the truth make you free (see John 8:32)?

7. What lies about yourself and others do you need to recognize and then replace with truths?

8. What new truths about God, yourself, and others do you need to embrace?

9. What feelings, thoughts, and behaviors alert you that your negative love style is in control? (When you recognize these, then you can refute them.) For example, alerts to avoider behavior might be isolating yourself, detaching emotionally, eluding eye contact, and being abnormally silent. Ask others to help you see when you are in the old pattern.

10. When two people with different love styles get married, predictable relational patterns occur. We will talk about these at length in the next section. Before you read on, try to identify the patterns within your marriage. Which patterns mentioned in *How We Love* do they match?

GROUP EXERCISES

11. Take turns sharing which imprint you identify with and why.
12. Address the spiritual implications of your imprint by discussing the beliefs that characterize your imprint that are distortions of the truth.
13. Talk about what kind of relational patterns might develop with the various combinations.

Part

Duets That Damage How We Love

Chapter 10

The Vacillator Marries the Avoider

When avoiders marry vacillators, the vacillators tend to pursue the independent spouse. When the avoiders instinctively disengage and retreat, the vacillators feel rebuffed and abandoned, and their anger intensifies. Over time, the chase scene picks up both speed and intensity, leading these couples on a perilous roller-coaster ride.

1. What traits initially attracted you to your spouse?

FOR THE AVOIDER

2. Do you feel as if you are constantly in trouble with your spouse? If so, what do you think you've said or done to be in trouble? Now think about your spouse's childhood history. In what specific ways was he or she disappointed by relationships in the past? Do you think your spouse could be feeling the same way as he or she relates to you? What impact could this insight have on your relationship?

FOR THE VACILLATOR

3. When did you become disappointed with your spouse? When did you realize that he or she has trouble connecting? Now review your spouse's childhood and explain why he or she has trouble connecting. What impact could this insight have on your relationship?

4. When you are angry, what kind of behavior and words do you direct at your spouse? Ephesians 4:26 says, "In your anger do not sin" (NIV). In what ways, if any, do you sin when you are angry?

5. Now consider the possibility that your spouse is getting some of the anger that someone in your past deserves. Who might that someone be, and what could have prompted your anger?

6. Every time you are mad, stop and ask yourself, What is the hurt under this anger? Once you figure it out, communicate that sad, hurt feeling to your spouse rather than the anger.

For the Avoider

7. Do you feel like you are walking on eggshells? Explain.

8. When your spouse gets angry, how do you feel inside? Do you remember having a similar feeling during your childhood years?

9. In an earlier question, your spouse was encouraged to learn to get sad, not mad. Tell your spouse you are willing to learn to comfort him or her, if he or she will work on the sad feelings. (Chapter 17 on engagement will help you do that.)

10. If you were willing to be less avoidant and allow your vacillator spouse's emotions, and if his or her anger diminished as a result, how might that change your negative marital dynamics? Would you be more inclined to be less avoidant? If so, in what ways?

For the Vacillator

11. If you were to become less angry and critical of your avoider spouse, how might this change your negative marital dynamics? Would you be more inclined to control your vacillations? If so, in what ways?

For Both of You

12. Review the workbook discussion of your particular imprint. Choose one growth goal to work on, and tell your spouse what it is. Write a prayer asking God to help you reach your goal.

13. If you're working with a group, share your growth goal with the members, and ask them to pray for you and hold you accountable.

The Pleaser Marries the Vacillator

Vacillators idealize pleasers' giving natures and believe they have found their soul mates. All is well until the vacillators' idealized view is shattered by disappointment, and they become angry. The pleasers' fear of that anger causes them to try harder, but they lose a bit of themselves in the process. After years of living out this pattern, pleasers walk on eggshells and are passively resentful. The vacillators are still unhappy, sensing a connection based on fear and duty rather than passion.

1. From *How We Love,* is there anything in Peter and Shannon's story or Michael and Sandy's story in chapter 11 that you relate to? If so, what?

2. What traits initially attracted you to your spouse?

FOR THE PLEASER

3. Do you feel as if you are constantly in trouble with your spouse? If so, what do you think you've said or done to be in trouble? Now think about your spouse's childhood history. In what specific ways was he or she disappointed by relationships in the past? Do you think your spouse could be feeling the same way as he or she relates to you? What impact could this insight have on your relationship?

FOR THE VACILLATOR

4. When did you become disappointed with your spouse? When did you realize that he or she has trouble connecting? Review your spouse's childhood and explain why he or she has trouble connecting. What impact could this insight have on your relationship?

5. When you are angry, what kind of behavior and words do you direct at your spouse? Ephesians 4:26 says, "In your anger do not sin" (NIV). In what ways, if any, do you sin when you are angry?

6. Now consider the possibility that your spouse is getting some of the anger that someone in your past deserves. Who might that someone be, and what could have prompted your anger?

7. Every time you are mad, stop and ask yourself, What is the hurt under this anger? Once you figure it out, communicate that sad, hurt feeling to your spouse rather than the anger.

FOR THE PLEASER

8. Do you as if you are walking on eggshells? Explain.

9. When your spouse gets angry, how do you feel inside? Do you remember having a similar feeling during your childhood years?

10. In an earlier question, your spouse was encouraged to learn to get sad, not mad. Tell your spouse you are willing to learn to comfort him or her. What frightens you about making this offer?

11. One more question about your reaction to your spouse's anger: Do you feel something inside other than fear, something like sadness and anger? Make an effort to be aware of feelings inside you besides anxiety and share them with your spouse. If he or she gets upset, you'll be able to practice owning your feelings even if your spouse is agitated by your emotions. Journal about any feelings that have never come out before.

FOR THE VACILLATOR

12. How do you think it would change your negative marriage pattern if you worked on changing your love style? Describe how you would feel if your spouse were stronger and could engage with your painful emotions instead of just pleasing you. Are you willing to let him or her stand up and have more of a voice in the relationship? And what would you like your response to be if your spouse were to stand up to you? (Standing up to you is necessary before your spouse can engage with you in a healthy way.)

FOR THE PLEASER

13. How would your negative marriage pattern change if you worked on being honest and not always pleasing? Describe how you would feel if your spouse were less angry at you and took some responsibility for your negative love style.

FOR BOTH OF YOU

14. Review the workbook discussion of your particular imprint. Choose one growth goal to work on, and tell your spouse what it is. Write a prayer asking God to help you reach your goal.

15. If you're working with a group, share your growth goal with the members, and ask them to pray for you and hold you accountable.

Chapter 12

The Controller Marries the Victim

In this combination, usually controllers marry people with the weaker victim style. As the relationship begins, the roles feel strangely familiar and yet different, because both parties believe they have finally escaped their childhood homes. But it does not take long for controllers to become angry, possessive, and dissatisfied. When overwhelmed or threatened with a loss of power, the controller rages and intimidates. The victim, whose esteem was decimated long ago, believes he or she is at fault. Drugs, alcohol, and other addictive behaviors often find their way into this home as a means of soothing the constant anxiety everyone feels.

1. Is there anything in Bill and Carlie's story or Leslie and Paul's story in chapter 12 of the book that you relate to? If so, what?

2. If this is your marital combination, what things initially attracted you to your spouse?

3. What things about your mate have been the hardest for you to accept or live with?

One of the keys to changing this core dynamic is for the controller and the victim to learn to listen and offer comfort to each other about their painful childhood memories. Take time to listen and get to know the child inside your mate.

FOR VICTIMS

4. Do you feel you are constantly in trouble with, and disappointing to, your spouse? When you review your spouse's childhood history, how was he or she hurt or disappointed by relationships? How might your spouse's early experiences be fueling his or her anger now? It is important for you to realize the anger is not about you, even though it is probably directed at you now.

5. Do you feel like you are walking on eggshells? How does your spouse's anger make you feel inside? Do you remember a similar feeling from your childhood years? What events or people made you afraid?

6. Do you feel something inside other than fear, such as sadness, anger, shame, or something else? Journal about the feelings inside that have never really come into the light. Perhaps, at a later date, when you feel safer, you can share these feelings with your spouse.

If you haven't yet, you need to realize you can never be good enough to keep your spouse from getting angry. Write below how your feelings might change if your spouse took responsibility for controlling his or her emotions. As you learn to resist the controller's black-and-white, extreme thinking, try to remember that this person was once a little child who felt overwhelmed and hopeless. You can have compassion; however, you cannot "fix" him or her. And if you feel threatened or fearful in any way, you need to seek professional counsel.

For Controllers

7. Do you display anger toward your spouse? How? Is it "out of bounds" when you consider the biblical guidelines in Ephesians 4:26?

8. Is your spouse getting some of the anger that someone in your past deserves? Every time you are mad, stop and ask yourself, What is the hurt under this anger? Communicate the sad hurt feeling to your spouse rather than the anger.

9. Have you ever considered that you make your spouse (and children) feel just like the abusive people in your childhood made you feel when you were young? Write about how you felt as a child when people were critical, mean, and angry. Does your anger cause the same feelings in others now?

10. Are you willing to deal with your anger instead of blaming others? Your core pattern cannot change until you accept how destructive this is to your marriage.

11. Would you respect your mate more if one day he or she was stronger and learned to have an adult voice and speak up to you? How does your mate's passivity fuel your contempt?

For Both of You

12. Commit yourself to one growth goal from the workbook for your attachment style that will begin to change this core pattern. Share your goal with your spouse. Write a prayer below asking God to specifically help you with this goal.

Controller

Victim

Group Exercise

13. Share your growth goal with your group and ask them to hold you accountable.

Chapter 13

The Avoider Marries the Pleaser

Pleasers' insecurity causes yet another relational chase scene, yet instead of anger being the motivator, as it is with vacillators, fear drives pleasers into a relentless pursuit of the independent avoiders' attention. The pleasers' neediness irritates avoiders, and they move farther away. As the avoiders detach, the pleasers' anxiety and fear increase, so the chase intensifies. And the pattern continues.

1. What traits initially attracted you to your spouse?

2. Which of your spouse's traits have been the hardest for you to accept or live with?

For the Avoider

3. Do you feel as if you are constantly being chased, pursued, or smothered by your spouse? What words and/or behaviors prompt those feelings? Do you feel that you are frequently disappointing your spouse? If so, explain.

4. Now think about your spouse's childhood history. In what specific ways was he or she disappointed by relationships in the past? Do you think your spouse could be feeling the same way as he or she relates to you? What impact could this insight have on your relationship?

FOR THE PLEASER

5. When did you become disappointed with your spouse? When did you realize that he or she has trouble connecting with you as an adult? Now review your spouse's childhood and explain why he or she has trouble connecting with people in general. Describe your thoughts and feelings about their childhood. What impact could this insight have on your relationship?

FOR THE AVOIDER

6. When you are angry, what kind of behavior and words do you direct at your spouse? Are you verbal and clear about your anger, or do you want to pull away and be quietly angry? Why do you think that's your way of being angry?

7. Consider the possibility that your spouse is receiving the anger that someone in your past deserves. Who might that someone be, and what could have prompted your anger?

8. Every time you are mad, stop and ask yourself, What is the hurt under this anger? Once you figure it out, communicate that sad, hurt feeling to your spouse rather than the anger.

FOR THE PLEASER

9. What are you anxious about in your marriage relationship? Do you find yourself trying to avoid rejection or keep your spouse close to you so that you feel better about yourself? What could be the roots of that behavior?

10. What do you feel when your spouse expresses the need for some time or space apart from you? Do you worry that, if you gave your spouse that space, he or she might never come back? What do you feel inside when you contemplate this? Again, what could be at the root of that concern?

11. When, if ever, have you felt sad that people moved away from you (either emotionally or physically)? Do you remember a similar feeling from your childhood years?

12. In an earlier question, we asked your spouse to learn to get sad rather than mad. Tell your spouse you are willing to learn to comfort him or her as well as be comforted when you are sad or scared. Does the idea of approaching your spouse in this way frighten you? Explain.

For the Avoider

13. How would the core pattern (the repetitive conflict that you experience) in your marriage change if you worked on changing your love style? Be specific.

For the Pleaser

14. How would the core pattern in your marriage change if you worked on changing your love style?

For Both of You

15. Review the workbook discussion of your particular love style. Choose one growth goal to work on, and tell your spouse what it is. Write a prayer asking God to help you reach your goal.

16. If you're working with a group, share your growth goal with the members, and ask them to pray for you and hold you accountable.

Chapter 14

Other Challenging Combinations

THE AVOIDER-AVOIDER COMBINATION

As we said in the book, "Pleasant talk and shared interests cause two avoiders to enjoy spending time together. Since both individuals are independent and self-sufficient, they may be satisfied with less contact than most dating couples find satisfactory. Long-distance relationships are also more acceptable to this combination, and usually the level of emotional connection between this pair is somewhat superficial because it is familiar and comfortable. Also, since neither partner is comfortable with emotional displays, this relationship is often even-keeled; the couple experiences few ups and downs. Not surprisingly, feelings are rarely the topic of conversations, but intellectual discussions about subjects of mutual interest may be quiet deep. If both people are introverts, each will value and maintain space, solitude, and privacy."

The following questions are for both of you.

1. What traits initially attracted you to your spouse?

2. Which of your spouse's traits have been the hardest for you to accept or live with?

3. Does either of you feel as if the two of you are just roommates, friends, or acquaintances? If so, do you feel a sense of loss about this? Explain why or why not.

4. When, if ever, do you feel lonely in the relationship?

5. Do you find it hard to communicate your loneliness to your spouse? Explain your feelings.

6. When you are angry, what kind of behavior and words do you direct at your spouse? Are you verbal and clear about your anger, quietly resentful, or gruff and abrupt with your mate? Why do you think that's your way of being angry?

7. Now consider the possibility that your spouse is getting some of the anger that someone in your past deserves. Who might that someone be, and what could have prompted your anger?

8. Every time you are mad, stop and ask yourself, What is the hurt under this anger? Once you figure it out, communicate that sad, hurt feeling to your spouse rather than the anger.

9. How would your relationship change if each of you worked at changing your love style?

10. Review the workbook discussion of your particular love style. Choose one growth goal to work on, and tell your spouse what it is. Write a prayer asking God to help you reach your goal.

11. If you're working in a group, share your growth goal with the members, and ask them to pray for you and hold you accountable.

THE VACILLATOR-VACILLATOR, CONTROLLER-VACILLATOR, OR CONTROLLER-CONTROLLER COMBINATIONS

From the book: "In all three of these combinations, two people who both need control are marrying each other. The resulting core patterns are similar, so we will talk about all three combinations together. When a couple like this meets, there is often an immediate strong and passionate connection. The chemistry seems to be just right, and the intense good feelings are a welcome relief from the pain of the past. The relationship is all good as long as the idealization phase lasts. Then it goes downhill with the same intensity."

12. What traits initially attracted you to your spouse?

13. Which of your spouse's traits have been the hardest for you to accept or live with?

14. Both of these love styles have tendencies to anger. If you are a vacillator or a controller, what kind of behavior and words do you direct at your spouse when you are angry? Ephesians 4:26 says, "In your anger do not sin" (NIV). In what ways, if any, do you sin when you are angry?

15. Now consider the possibility that your spouse is getting some of the anger that someone in your past deserves. Who might that someone be, and what could have prompted your anger?

16. Every time you are mad, stop and ask yourself, What is the hurt under this anger? Once you figure it out, communicate that sad, hurt feeling to your spouse rather than the anger.

17. Think about your spouse's childhood history. In what specific ways was he or she disappointed by relationships in the past? Do you think your spouse could be feeling the same way as he or she relates to you? What impact could this insight have on your relationship?

18. Take turns, with open minds, to ask your spouse what he or she feels when around you?

19. How would your marriage change if each of you worked on changing your love style?

20. Review the workbook discussion of your particular love style. Choose one growth goal to work on, and tell your spouse what it is. Write a prayer asking God to help you reach your goal.

21. If you're working with a group, share your growth goal with the members, and ask them to pray for you and hold you accountable.

Part

4

Changing How
We Love

Chapter 15

The Comfort Circle

While we can't control the way we were raised, we can control how we choose to live the rest of our lives. The key to having healthier relationships, and therefore a happier life, is escaping the gravitational field of our negative imprints of intimacy. Thankfully, that's what God's life-transforming power is all about. He is in the business of making us new creations and forming in us new relational imprints—if we let Him.

EXTRA HELP IN BREAKING YOUR CORE PATTERN

1. Sometimes childhood roles can contribute to the core pattern of a marriage. In chapter 3 of the workbook, you identified roles you may have played in your childhood home. Which of these roles, if any, do you play in your marriage? In what ways have they influenced your core pattern?

As we are growing up, we all adopt certain defenses to protect ourselves against conflict and relational pain. These defenses can be found listed in any basic psychology book and are common to everyone. Review the list below and put a check mark beside those that might be your preferences.

_____ *Regression:* "If I am angry or hurt, sometime I act in childish ways. I pout, sulk, go to my parents' house, or have temper tantrums."

_____ *Suppression:* "I distract myself a lot so I don't have to feel or deal with what is bothering me. I can practically erase unpleasant experiences."

_____ *Withdrawal:* "When I'm hurt or upset, I physically leave, or I just go off in my own thoughts."

_____ *Blame:* "Other people cause most of my problems. I act and feel the way I do because of them. If they would change, everything would be fine." (This is a very common choice.)

_____ *Rationalization:* "It's easy to tell myself the wrong things I do aren't that bad when I compare myself to what most of the people in the world do wrong." (This choice is a close second after blame.)

_____ *Devaluation:* "When I'm upset, I focus on the negative traits of others. Those traits are always more numerous and pronounced than my own."

_____ *Intellectualization:* "I can analyze my way out of any feeling or emotion."

_____ *Compensation:* "I feel the need to exaggerate my good points in order to hide any deficiencies."

_____ *Denial:* "I refuse to acknowledge pain and problems and call it having a positive attitude."

_____ *Replacement:* "When I'm feeling a negative emotion, I express the opposite in order to hide the truth."

_____ *Distraction:* "I avoid conflict or pain by filling the day with anything and everything."

2. Which of these behaviors and attitudes are surfacing in your marriage? What happened—or might have happened—during your childhood to cause you to develop these defenses? Write out your ideas.

Defenses block pain. In contrast, acknowledging and being willing to *feel* the pain reduces the need for protective armor. Processing pain and finding comfort and relief through relationships will leave us more open and free to relate to people, including our spouses, in non-defensive ways.

3. What is one specific response or action you can implement that might help you to begin to let go of your defenses the next time you find yourself using them?

4. It is difficult to change or let go of a behavior or attitude if we don't have an alternative behavior or attitude in mind. What attitude(s) or behavior(s) might *replace* your defensive postures? For example, if you use denial as a defense, what specific steps can you take when you notice you are in denial?

5. Sometimes core patterns surface when our spouses remind us of our parent(s) and we react in the same way without realizing what we're doing. (Some of these reminders might be referred to as "triggers.") Which of your spouse's expectations, behaviors, attitudes, or tones of voice, if any, remind you of one of your parents? Are you reacting to your spouse in the same way you reacted to your parent(s) when you were a child or teen? Be specific. Is your reaction part of a repetitive pattern in your marriage? If so, consider that your reaction might be connected to past experiences and why that truth is significant for your marriage relationship.

CORE PATTERN WORKSHEET

6. What repetitive fight or pattern of fighting, if any, do you experience in your marriage relationship? Describe it.

7. What events, feelings, behaviors, actions, expectations, or tones of voice trigger the pattern?

8. What are your behaviors in this pattern? What are your feelings and thoughts as you live out this pattern?

9. When you're living out this pattern, what beliefs are you acting on about yourself? about your spouse? about God?

10. What are your most intense feelings when this pattern occurs?

11. What message, expectation, behavior, attitude, or tone of voice when you relate to your spouse is similar to what you knew with your parent(s)? Explain.

12. When you were a child, how did you react to authority figures who were negative toward you? How do you react now when your spouse does something similar?

13. In what specific way(s) did this imprint, role, defense mechanism, behavior, or attitude help or protect you as a child? Did your role, for example, help improve your mom's mood or did your defense mechanism keep you from feeling your dad's anger?

14. When this pattern occurs, how does it hinder intimacy and the expression of love in your marriage?

15. Share your insights with your spouse or group.

16. Put a check mark beside the following myths and misconceptions about marriage that you identify with. Counter each one with a true statement—and know that the truth may not be what you want to hear!

_____ "You shouldn't have to work on *true* love."

_____ "Our positive attitude/motivation/skill/compatibility will keep us going."

_____ "Christians should just claim victory over their marriage problems."

_____ "I shouldn't have to change; my mate should love me just the way I am."

_____ "I keep trying to get my spouse to change, but he or she won't budge!"

_____ "I'd be happier with another person. I just know my soul mate is out there."

_____ "If the feelings are gone, there's no hope."

_____ "If I were honest with my mate, I don't think he or she could handle it."

_____ "When God decides to change my feelings, then I will change."

_____ "My spouse should know what I need and do it!"

17. Review the following reasons relational problems develop. Discuss the ones that have had the strongest impact on your marriage.
    - inadequate modeling and teaching
    - hurt and pain from your family of origin
    - roles or defense mechanisms you learned in childhood that protected you then but now block and hinder intimacy
    - a restricted range of emotions (feelings indicate needs, so if you don't know what you feel or if you only have a narrow range of emotions, you won't know what you need)
    - wrong priorities (focusing too much on children or work/career to the detriment of your marriage)
    - seasons of intense stress that push character weaknesses to the forefront
    - a relationship in which conflict is not resolved in a healthy way; such conflict produces resentment, bitterness, anger, and the tendency to see your spouse as the problem

All the negative coping mechanisms we've just described are ways we miss the mark before a holy God. We all fail and have shortcomings that sabotage our relationships. When we do, we find ourselves outside His will for our lives, where we face problems and consequences that often make us miserable. The Bible calls this sowing and reaping. If you are in a group, discuss your thoughts as to how you have been outside God's will and in what ways you might be reaping what you have been sowing.

18. The way of healing and bonding is to reverse all of these wayward tendencies in your relationship with God and others. Look at the comfort circle on the next page and read the steps with your spouse. Is that person willing to go around the comfort circle with you? If not, are you willing to focus on yourself and begin to change and grow as an individual? If not, why not? Also, are you willing to take the role of listener for a while in order to try to draw out your spouse's thoughts and feelings about love, life, and the hope of change?

Before moving on to the next section, review the following key concepts about comfort:

- Important relationships are *dynamic,* not *static.* They are ever-changing and must be continually maintained.
- Every time you successfully complete a circle, you'll experience greater trust and security, a blossoming love, and the elevation of your relationship to a higher plane.
- When couples cannot go around this circle, their relationship steadily declines and deteriorates.

19. When you were growing up, was any member of your family able to go around this comfort circle with you? If so, who? What impact did this connection have on you? If no one comforted you, at what point on the circle did your family get stuck? What impact has this lack of experience in comfort had on your ability to communicate in your marriage?

The Comfort Circle

1. Seek Awareness
of feelings and underlying needs.

4. Resolve
needs verbally and with touch,
seeking how and when needs
may be met in the future.

2. Engage
with feelings and
acknowledge needs openly.

3. Explore
the speaker's thoughts and feelings—
listening, validating, and concluding
with, "What do you need?"

Note: Completing the circle should bring relief—an increase in trust and feelings of connectedness. If hurtful action or inaction is experienced at any point in the circle, you should begin again.

20. If you're in a group, take turns discussing your childhood experiences and what part of the circle will be most challenging for you.

As we said at the beginning of the chapter, we cannot change the state of a fallen and sinful world or our experience in it, but with God's help we can learn new attitudes and behaviors that will create a *new imprint of intimacy* within our minds and hearts—one that more closely resembles a healthy and secure love style. By starting new practices, leaving behind lies we've believed, and realigning our attitudes, we will learn to become bonded to those people who are most important to us. It is a conscious choice, and the effort required can feel like boot camp. In fact, in some ways it feels like we are growing up all over again. Know that growing in this way can have a dramatic impact on the level of intimacy in your marriage. The potential rewards are worth the effort.

Chapter 16

Seek Awareness

Healing and reconciliation can only begin when we are willing to take responsibility for our part in the unhealthy marriage dance. Husbands and wives usually blame each other. In fact, they are often blind to their own injurious imprints. We begin walking the path of acceptance, confession, and forgiveness when we admit before God and others the ways that our harmful imprints contribute to the problems in our marriages.

The starting point is simply becoming aware of a single thought or feeling in your mind and soul. It could be something that makes you happy or sad. It could be an emotion that is distressing or perhaps quite soothing. It might be a warm thought about your spouse, or it might be just the opposite. You might be irritated because of something he or she has done. Many people feel emotions but have no words with which to define those emotions for themselves, let alone to tell someone else about what they're feeling.

Use the soul words list to help you answer the following questions:

1. What are a few of the feelings on this list that you most often feel?

2. What feelings do you think your spouse most commonly feels?

3. What do you most rarely feel?

4. What feelings do you rarely see your spouse express?

5. What feelings would be most frightening for you to express? Why?

6. What feelings do you believe your spouse would have the most difficult time expressing?

7. What feelings would be most difficult to see or hear your spouse express? Why?

8. What do you wish you could feel more often?

9. What do you wish your spouse could feel more often? Why?

10. Pick three words from the soul words list to describe your current feelings about the following, then have a feelings talk with your spouse about your answers.

marriage

friendships

job

children

church

finances

11. What has answering these questions taught you about yourself? What feelings on the list would you not have identified if you hadn't seen them in print? Why would using this list on a regular basis help you become more aware of your feelings?

12. Draw two circles to represent the tanks described in the book. Label one *Fuel* and the second one *Pressure.* Draw a line to indicate how full each of your tanks is right now. Then, next to each tank, list some things that would help fill the fuel tank or empty the pressure tank. Share your answers with your spouse.

13. When was the last time you filled up your spouse's fuel tank with praise or appreciation? What would help this encouragement happen more often? Write down some ideas and start acting today.

GROUP EXERCISE

14. What feelings on the soul words list are most often expressed in your group? Which emotions are rarely expressed? Which feelings do you wish members in your group would express more freely? What would have to happen for that kind of sharing to be safe?

15. This week ask different people how they feel about something. Listen to see if you get a feeling word or facts. If you get facts, ask again for a feeling. Note your experiences.

Extra Help with Triggers

16. After reading about triggers in the book, take a moment to think about anything you might consider a trigger. Then write a prayer asking God to help you better manage those areas of reactivity. If you're having trouble identifying your triggers, ask God to help you identify them.

17. In *How We Love* we suggested that, when you notice yourself feeling intense reactions to something or someone (even if others don't notice), you take a deep breath, settle down, and ask yourself three questions: (a) When have I felt this in the past? (b) Who was I with? (c) What soul words describe this intense reaction? Walk through that process now and write your answers below.

18. Which of your spouse's behaviors, attitudes, reactions, or tones of voice cause strong feelings in you?

19. When have you felt these same strong feelings in the past?

20. Who were you with when you felt these same intense feelings?

21. What soul words describe this intense reaction in the present? And to whom from your past would you like to be able to tell what you were feeling? Remember, we don't suggest that you actually say these words to family members.

22. Write a paragraph about the childhood experiences that underlie your triggers. If you can't think of anything, come back to this question later.

23. Your spouse's behavior may be genuinely irritating, but explain why your old injury causes your current feelings to be more powerful. What, for instance, did you do or not do with those feelings in the past?

24. Not focusing on your mate when you are triggered is hard, but we encourage you to do so by sharing with him or her the real origin of your pain.

25. Perhaps your spouse could be more sensitive in your trigger areas. What changes in his or her behavior and attitudes would soften, if not eliminate, your triggers? Write ideas about what might help and share them with your spouse.

If you find yourself getting angry at your parents as you consider the impact of the past on the present, remember that they entered marriage and parenting with their own childhood injuries and human shortcomings. So don't express your anger to them. Instead, role play. Have your spouse or a friend sit in for the parent or relative you are upset with and talk to that person in the present tense as though you were speaking to your relative.

26. At the end of chapter 16 on awareness in *How We Love,* we shared how people with each imprint might struggle to become aware of certain feelings. Read the section on your imprint. Do you agree with what we wrote? If so, write a growth goal below to help expand your range of emotions. If not, explain why.

Chapter 17

Engage

Remember how Adam and Eve fearfully hid from God after disobeying him? Our natural tendency is to do the same—to hide in fear when we are troubled. Such shame, however, causes us to hold many thoughts and feelings within. Consequently, we suffer in silence as we isolate ourselves; we stay alone in our pain. God, however, tells us to step into the light of relationship and to bring our inner thoughts and feelings into community.

Many of us were not welcomed into relationships when our feelings were not positive. So we learned to be quiet. Now that we're adults, we either hold everything in, or we dump our feelings onto others in hurtful, blaming ways. But God calls all of us to lay aside our fears and shame and to engage with other people. This can be very hard to do, especially if we never had opportunities to do so or positive experiences when we were growing up.

So engagement can feel frightening, yet the goal is to bring the newly discovered feelings, thoughts, and reactions out from the hidden recesses of our souls and into the open light of relationship. God wants to engage with us and help us grow. He is in the business of mending our wounds and giving us a new song in our mouths (see Psalm 40:3). Marriage is one of the primary places where He shines His light on our childish ways in order to help us grow.

1. What were your feelings and responses as you read about Kay's response to her miscarriage in chapter 17 of *How We Love*?

2. What was your reaction to the poem "The Wall" on pages 231–32 in *How We Love*? In what details did you see yourself and/or your marriage?

3. Are you a better giver or a better receiver? Why do you think you're that way?

4. Are you a giver in your marriage? Rate yourself on a scale from 1 to 10. Write about a recent time when you noticed the needs of your spouse and worked on meeting them (engaging) without being asked.

5. When, if at all, did you recently notice a need but chose to ignore it in hope it would go away? Why do you think you responded that way?

6. Are you willing to sacrifice in order to meet your spouse's needs if it takes more time and effort than you expected? Or do you just give up when meeting a need gets too hard? Explain what might be the root of that behavior.

7. If your mate is unresponsive and unappreciative when you give to him or her, do you keep trying anyway? Why or why not?

8. Make it your goal to give to your spouse in one specific way this week. Below, note his or her reaction.

9. On a scale of 1 to 10, rate yourself as a receiver. Why do you think it is hard or easy for you to receive?

10. Are you open to having your spouse help you recognize your shortcomings? Will you allow him or her to expose an area of need? Why or why not?

11. Do you need your spouse only in superficial ways (tasks and duties), or do you reveal to him or her your deeper soul needs? Give evidence supporting your answer and explain why you share the needs you do.

12. When someone gives you a compliment, can you accept it? Why or why not?

13. Can you accept compliments, praise, or appreciation from your spouse if he or she also has a valid criticism in another area, or does the criticism cancel out the compliment? What do you think that is all about?

14. Will you admit your frailties to your spouse and confess to him or her that you need to be loved in your most unlovely places? Confessing our weaknesses and shortcomings makes room for our spouses to offer us the love we need.

15. When your spouse tries wholeheartedly to open his or her arms and heart to you, do you accept that love, or do you act based on your resentment for past mistakes and keep your mate at a distance? Explain your behavior as best you can.

16. Do you feel that your spouse is an enemy? If so, why? And if so, are you willing to draw up a truce? Tell them about it and ask them to start over with you. Write the results of your efforts.

17. Describe the most recent time you apologized or confessed your sin to your mate.

18. When you were growing up, how did your family handle apologies, mistakes, and hurtful behavior? In what specific ways has that childhood experience influenced you?

19. For what attitude or behavior do you need to apologize to someone? What's keeping you from doing so? Ask your spouse or a friend to support you by praying and holding you accountable. Then go apologize.

20. Evaluate the level of honesty in your marriage. Is it satisfactory? Why or why not? What steps would improve the level of honesty?

21. What do you fear about telling the truth? What do you think your spouse's reaction to the truth would be?

22. Some common secrets that spouses keep from each other are sexual struggles within the marriage or outside the marriage, matters of finances and spending, relationships outside

the marriage that put the marriage at risk, addictions, and sharing with others things one mate has told the other in confidence. Are you keeping secrets from your spouse? What negative impact could that be having on your relationship? Consider the implications of having those secrets revealed. Would confessing or getting caught be better for your marriage? Perhaps you need to share your responses with someone like your pastor or a close friend before you share them with your spouse.

23. As long as we hide, nothing in us or our relationship can change. Write some topics you would like to tell the truth about. Why are you hiding each item you listed? What might be the long-term consequences of not telling the truth?

24. Are you taking charge of your own change and growth, or do you think your mate should just accept you as you are? Have you seen a weakness in your life but done nothing about it? What effect do you think that has on your spouse? Spend some time in prayer asking God to soften your heart so you will engage more fully with your mate and in your journey of growth. (You do want your marriage to improve, don't you?)

25. Think about the safety pyramid. Is anyone (ideally your spouse) at the top of your pyramid? Why or why not? If your spouse is not at the point of your pyramid, what would have to change for him or her to be a safe person for you?

26. Plan a fun date (follow the suggestions on page 12 of this book) and write about how it went.

27. Do you make an effort to learn from your spouse? Write about the last time your spouse's ideas changed your point of view. What strengths does your spouse have that complement yours?

28. At the end of chapter 17 on engagement in *How We Love,* we discussed how people with each imprint might struggle to engage. Read the section about your imprint. Do you agree with what we wrote? If so, write a growth goal for yourself about how you could be a better engager. If you see your struggle as different from what we describe, describe your experience. What could your spouse do that would help you engage more readily?

GROUP EXERCISE

Discuss the qualities you look for in people that make you willing to dialoging openly with them. Share with the group your own strengths and weaknesses in engaging with others, as well as one attitude or behavior you would like to improve in this area.

TIPS FOR ENGAGING WITH OTHER LOVE STYLES

Pleasers: Pleasers fear rejection. When you engage with pleasers, reassure them that your complaints don't mean you don't love them. Encourage them to be truthful with you. Tell them that even if you are hurt or angry, your marriage can and will survive. Also ask pleasers to speak directly about what is bothering them.

Avoiders: Don't take their distancing personally. They are just doing what they learned to do. Be patient with their efforts to put their feelings into words because this is a new experience for them. Ask them questions, and then be quiet and give them time to think. If you get only facts, ask them to use a feeling word so you can better understand their experiences. If avoiders engage with you and ask you to meet a need, realize what a huge step that was and appreciate their efforts.

Vacillators: Instead of avoiding engagement with vacillators, sit them down and tell them some things you love and appreciate about them. Touch them as you are sharing. Explain that the purpose of this engagement is for you to express your thoughts and feelings with them. If they bring up problems, promise to listen at another time—and be sure to keep your promise.

Controllers: Take a deep breath and approach controllers directly yet calmly. Remember that when threatened or intimidated, controllers feel the need to control. They do not have well-developed coping mechanisms, so stick with one topic, keep the number of words to a minimum, and give them time to formulate a response. Smile, touch, and reassure controllers that you will be patient with them if they engage in ways that also make you feel safe. If they start to become volatile, tell them you are taking a brief time-out while they think. Come back in a few minutes to finish.

Victims: Victims are scared when anyone approaches them in a direct manner. As you engage with them, smile and reassure them that you want to connect with them in a positive way. Use a calm, quiet voice and speak slowly and deliberately. If you can, sit in a position lower than they are (like on the floor if they are on a sofa). Don't stare at them; instead, avert your gaze and look at them directly only occasionally and for short periods. Tell them they can have all the time they need to formulate their responses. Keep the entire engagement short at first, because it will be uncomfortable for them.

Chapter 18

Explore

God's desire is that we be "quick to hear, slow to speak and slow to anger" (James 1:19). Healing and growth can begin when we are willing to listen and learn the art of extended listening. This chapter will help you learn to listen attentively instead of reacting defensively.

God calls us to "speak truth each one of you with his neighbor, for we are members of one another" (Ephesians 4:25). When we obey this verse, we bring out into the open the inner truths we have become aware of. We risk bringing our thoughts and feelings into relationship. When we openly acknowledge our feelings—when we bring that truth into the light—healing begins. The festering, old thoughts and feelings that contaminate our souls are flushed out, allowing fresh new thoughts and feelings to occur.

Sadly, too many of us have souls that are like the Dead Sea: it has no natural outlet and cannot sustain life. When water can flow, a lake stays fresh and can sustain life. Our souls also need an outflow if we are to know life and vitality. Opening up our hearts and sharing our thoughts will start that much-needed cleansing flow.

1. The Bible has so much to say about how we communicate. Look up the following verses and note what they say about your prayer and thought life as well as how you talk with others.

   Psalm 51:6

   Psalm 139:23–24

   Proverbs 16:23

THE SPEAKER

Goal: to explore a topic in a way that minimizes defensiveness in the listener. We need to speak truth in an edifying way (see Ephesians 4:25–32).

Getting Started

- Clearly state your desire to talk about one specific topic (for example, "I need to talk to you about the monthly finances"). Don't hint ("Maybe we could spend some time together") and don't drop bombs ("Well, the bank is going to repossess the house this month").
- Check the listener's readiness to listen ("When would be a good time for you to discuss this?") and agree upon a time.

Tips

- Introduce the issue you'd like to discuss by talking about yourself, your experiences, and your feelings.
- Use *I* statements rather than *you* statements. "I am feeling sad that I didn't get to spend any time with you" will be more easily heard than "You are always busy and never have time for me." If you need to share something negative about the listener, start and end with a positive affirmation about him or her.
- If the listener is causing you to feel unsafe, share what is making you feel unsafe: "I am feeling unsafe because your tone of voice sounds disinterested and defensive."
- If you have a concern about how the talk might go, share that concern at the beginning: "I have something to share that is difficult for me. Please try to hear me out."
- Use soul words to explain your experience.
- Be honest. Pretending or minimizing is dishonest. Speak the truth in the most loving way you can.
- Be vulnerable. Try not to avoid pain or embarrassment that may be a part of sharing deep feelings.

  If you get angry, take a time-out, but don't use it as a way to escape or avoid. Statements like this work well: "I'm getting so angry that I need to call a time-out so I can cool down. We'll continue this talk in ten minutes." Do not blame, accuse, or call the listener names.

Proverbs 17:27

Proverbs 18:2

Proverbs 19:19–20

Proverbs 20:5

THE LISTENER

Goal: to gain the speaker's perspective on a situation by asking questions about feelings, thoughts, and experiences (see James 1:19–20).

Getting Started
- Listen calmly. Don't defend yourself, argue, explain, or try to problem solve. You don't have to agree with what you are hearing in order to learn.
- Focus on the speaker's experience, *not* yours.

Tips
- Control defensiveness. Do not react. Pay attention to your nonverbal responses. Remember that when your defenses go up, the quality of your listening goes down. Know that you can listen with an open mind even if you disagree with what you're hearing. The speaker is a separate person with his or her own feelings, thoughts, personality, and family history. Your spouse's perspective is different from yours.
- Don't roll your eyes, sigh, groan, or respond in other ways that stop communication.
- Maintain eye contact and encourage the speaker to continue.

The Four Keys of Listening
1. Ask the speaker to stop periodically so you can summarize what you're hearing.

Nehemiah 5:6–7

Ephesians 4:25–27

James 1:19–20

James 3:1–18

---

2. Repeat in your own words what you heard, and check for accuracy.

3. Ask questions that will increase your understanding.

4. Respond with empathy: "I see what you are saying" or "I can see how you might feel that way."

Listening Questions

- Don't ask why. This is often accusatory and difficult to answer.
- "Tell me more. I want to understand." (Say this whenever you are stuck.)
- "How does that make you feel?" or "How long have you been feeling this way?"
- "Do you feel anything in addition to what you just shared?"
- "Are there other times you have felt this way? When was that?"
- "What are your hopes? your expectations? your desires?"
- "On a scale of 1 to 10, how strong is your feeling?"
- "I can tell you are really upset. Do you think something triggered these intense emotions?"
- "If you could share what you're feeling right now with someone in the present or the past, who would it be? What would you say to that person?"
- "Does what you're currently feeling remind you of an old or familiar feeling that you felt when you were growing up?"
- "What does you body feel like right now?"
- "What do you need?" (Use this as your closing question.)

2. Pages 135–37 are summary sheets for the roles of speaker and listener. Make a copy of each and a copy of the soul words list too. Use these when you have a conversation with your spouse. They will help you stay on track.

———

Conversations about problems between you and your spouse are among the most challenging ones you'll face. So as you get used to the listener and speaker roles, pick a topic that does not involve negative feelings about your spouse. Childhood memories (good or bad) are a good choice, because your spouse will learn more about you as, together, you work your way around the circle. *The only way to learn this skill is to try it.* If the pace is slow, you are on the right track. There will be pauses as the listener thinks of good questions and as the speaker reflects on his or her thoughts and feelings. Choose one of the "Conversation Starters" on page 258 of *How We Love.*

3. If anger makes it difficult to communicate with your spouse, practice saying a time-out statement to each other when you are *not* having an argument. Note below what happens the first time you actually use a time-out statement.

4. Is your spouse an introvert or are there introverts in your family? Ask introverts you know if they tend to feel interrupted and talked over in their conversations with people. When talking with introverts, make an effort to ask a question and wait for an answer, no matter how long it takes for them to answer.

5. Here is a fun exercise to help you and your spouse learn to validate each other even when you disagree. Sit with your spouse and take turns making statements that you know he

or she will disagree with. The listener will practice validating the speaker's point of view even though they disagree. For example:

- "I can understand how you could feel that way."
- "From your perspective, your feelings make sense."
- "I would probably feel the same way if I were in your shoes."
- "It makes sense to me that you would feel…"

Sometimes people get flustered when their mates are emotional during conversations. A good way to react when your spouse shows emotions is simply to say what you see: "I can see you are really hurt" or "I can see how upset this makes you." Comments like this let your mate know you are aware of his emotions and in tune with his feelings.

Also, try to maintain gentle physical contact (like a touch on the knee) with the speaker during the conversation. This is especially important if the person is obviously distraught (such as crying). However, if the speaker is really angry (especially if angry at you), she may not want to be touched, so give her some space. If softening and tears begin to occur, ask her if you may touch her or hold her hand.

6. At the end of chapter 18, we discussed how people with each imprint might struggle to be listeners and speakers (see pages 258–60). Read the section about your imprint. Do you agree with what we wrote? Whether you agree or disagree, what do you find most challenging about being a listener? a speaker? Write down your growth goals.

GROUP EXERCISE

7. Have a volunteer couple go around the comfort circle while the rest of the group watches and offers feedback. This exercise can be a bit intimidating for all involved, but it is one of the best ways to grow in your listening skills.

Chapter 19

Resolve

The question "What do you need?" can elicit a wide variety of responses. Different people need different things to help them feel better, and the last point in the comfort circle is to identify your spouse's best choice.

After compassionate and extended listening, you are ready to ask, "What do you need?" Doing so takes the guesswork and stress out of trying to come up with something on your own. It eliminates having to read your spouse's mind (an impossible task), and it requires your spouse to define his or her own needs. When it's clearly communicated, your spouse's answer gives you a very high chance of successfully meeting that need.

1. In the book I (Milan) talked about an experience where I processed some feelings alone on an airplane and felt relief. What are some ways you find relief alone?

2. What unhealthy ways of making negative feelings go away do you have, if any?

3. Do you tend to problem solve before listening? Does your spouse? What is the other person's reaction to that attempt to help? What would each speaker find more helpful than problem solving? If you don't know, ask!

4. Below are some important ways that a couple can experience resolution with each other. As you read each one, evaluate yourself and your spouse according to the three assessments listed first.

   (a) *I often say this. / My spouse often says this.*
   (b) *I rarely say this. / My spouse rarely says this.*
   (c) *I should say this more often. / My spouse should say this more often.*

   Ownership: "I admit and own the problem, infraction, or mistake."

   Forgiveness: "I offer a well-thought-out request for forgiveness and a genuine apology."

Expression of needs: "You know, I don't think I need anything right now. I just feel better having gotten that off my chest."

Reassurance: "I need to hear from you that things will be okay, that you will work on this, that you still really love me."

Agree to disagree: "While we still don't agree on this, I do feel like we understand each other's perspective."

Negotiation: "I need for us to find some middle ground or some kind of compromise."

Analysis and problem solving: "Would you help me figure out how to solve this recurring problem or fix this situation?"

Comfort and nurture: "Would you please hold me and comfort me?"

5. Are you able to apologize when you are wrong? If owning your mistakes and apologizing are hard for you, what impact on your marriage would developing these skills have?

6. Do you hold grudges and let resentments fester? Read Galatians 5:15, Ephesians 4:31–32, and Hebrews 12:14–15. What is the message for you?

7. When has God brought you comfort in a way you did not expect? Share an example or two.

8. Rate your ability to comfort your spouse. Describe a time when you feel as if you did well and a time when you could have done better.

9. Now rate your marriage in the area of nonsexual touch. What change, if any, would you like to see in this aspect of your relationship? Explain.

10. Remember Zach and Emily from chapter 19 of *How We Love*? What was your reaction to their story? Do you and your spouse have a hard time in the area of sexual desire differences? What did you think about Zach and Emily's compromise?

11. Comforter/Giver: Your goal as the comforter is to acknowledge and pursue your spouse when he or she is hurting, offer to be present both emotionally and physically, and validate the reality of his or her inner experiences through caring touch and support. How do you feel about offering to hold your spouse when he or she is hurting? What internal hesitation, if any, do you feel? What's that reluctance about, and what can you do to counter it?

12. Receiver: To receive comfort, you must first acknowledge and identify your feelings of pain. Then you must choose to be vulnerable and share this with your spouse, asking him or her to hold and comfort you. How do you feel about asking your spouse to hold you when you are hurting? How do you feel about offering to hold your spouse when he

or she is hurting? What internal hesitation, if any, do you feel? What's that reluctance about, and what can you do to counter it?

13. Which of the following common obstacles to giving and receiving comfort do you struggle with, if any? What can you do to remove those obstacles from your mind and/or heart?

- wanting and trying to fix the situation, problem solve, or troubleshoot the issue
- impatience and an unwillingness to stop whatever you're doing to engage with another's emotions
- aversion to emotions; fear of feelings and tears
- you have never experienced comfort

14. In light of your answers to questions 11, 12, and 13, are you willing to try a holding time with your mate (see pages 272–78 of *How We Love*)? Why or why not? If you're up for it, first try holding time without talking. Hold your spouse for five minutes or so. Before you switch places, describe your experience as the giver or receiver of comforting touch. Then switch places and be sure to debrief afterward. (If you're new to this, it may help to write out your initial feelings rather than speaking them aloud.)

Remember the comfort question: can you recall being comforted as a child or adolescent after a time of emotional distress? If your answer was no, which is the answer most people give, then you never experienced the emotional connection that God intends for you. *Now is your chance* to learn comfort as the giver and receiver.

As you grow more comfortable with holding your spouse and being held by him or her, you can try to be available like that for each other when one of you is hurting. Learning to be with people in their pain and comforting them when they are upset brings about new, wonderful levels of bonding and connection. Life always has its stresses, and we need to learn how to comfort each other when we face difficulties.

15. What impact would your ability to comfort each other have on your sexual relationship? Which activity makes you feel most vulnerable: having sex, receiving comfort, or giving comfort? Did your answer surprise you? What do you think it means?

GROUP EXERCISE

16. Discuss your feelings about holding time. When you do, you'll learn that you aren't the only one who feels awkward trying something new.

Chapter 20

Seeing into Your Spouse's Soul

Discuss the following questions with your spouse and/or group as a way to help you solidify the growth you've experienced through the use of these books.

1. What idea, suggestion, or exercise in this book has been most helpful to you?

2. What have you found most challenging about reading the book and doing this workbook?

3. What is the most important thing you have learned about yourself in this process?

4. What is the most important thing you have learned about your spouse?

5. What were your thoughts and feelings about how you have learned to love each other in your worst places?

6. In what worst place of your character or past do you most need your spouse to love and accept you?

7. Every small step of growth changes how you love. How are you loving your spouse differently after reading this book? Be specific.

CHANGING HOW WE LOVE

It has been nineteen short years since God brought into our lives the people who would help us uncover the roots of our marital struggles. We believe they were an answer to our prayer, one that has been spoken in our home more than any other. It consists of four simple words: "Lord, give us wisdom" (see James 1:5). It's a handy little prayer that fits into every day, because wisdom is needed for big and small things alike. One of our favorite passages is Philippians 1:9–10, which asks for a specific kind of wisdom:

> So this is my prayer: that your love will flourish and that you will not only love much but well. Learn to love appropriately. You need to use your head and test your feelings so that your love is sincere and intelligent, not sentimental gush. Live a lover's life, circumspect and exemplary, a life Jesus will be proud of: bountiful in fruits from the soul, making Jesus Christ attractive to all, getting everyone involved in the glory and praise of God. (MSG)

The writer of this passage isn't talking about trying harder to love. It's a request for a *greater capacity* to give and receive love based on deeper insight. Since making this our prayer, God has shown us more ways to better love each other than we ever expected.

We pray that *How We Love* and this workbook have been a guide to you and introduced you to a new dance of a deeper, richer relationship. Practicing these new steps that God designed will truly change how you love.

SOUL WORDS

HAPPY, cheerful, delighted, elated, encouraged, glad, gratified, joyful, light-hearted, overjoyed, pleased, relieved, satisfied, thrilled, secure

LOVING, affectionate, cozy, passionate, romantic, sexy, warm, tender, responsive, thankful, appreciative, refreshed, pleased

HIGH ENERGY, energetic, enthusiastic, excited, playful, rejuvenated, talkative, pumped, motivated, driven, determined, obsessed

AMAZED, stunned, surprised, shocked, jolted

ANXIOUS, uneasy, embarrassed, frustrated, nauseated, ashamed, nervous, restless, worried, stressed

CONFIDENT, positive, secure, self-assured, assertive

PEACEFUL, at ease, calm, comforted, cool, relaxed, serene

AFRAID, scared, anxious, apprehensive, boxed in, burdened, confused, distressed, fearful, frightened, guarded, hard pressed, overwhelmed, panicky, paralyzed, tense, terrified, worried, insecure

TRAUMATIZED, shocked, disturbed, injured, damaged

ANGRY, annoyed, controlled, manipulated, furious, grouchy, grumpy, irritated, provoked, frustrated

LOW ENERGY, beaten down, exhausted, tired, weak, listless, depressed, detached, withdrawn, indifferent, apathetic

ALONE, avoidant, lonely, abandoned, deserted, forlorn, isolated, cut off, detached

SAD, unhappy, crushed, dejected, depressed, desperate, despondent, grieved, heartbroken, heavy, weepy

BETRAYED, deceived, fooled, duped, tricked

CONFUSED, baffled, perplexed, mystified, bewildered

ASHAMED, guilty, mortified, humiliated, embarrassed, exposed

To learn more about WaterBrook Press and view
our catalog of products, log on to our Web site:
www.waterbrookpress.com

24280148R00095

Made in the USA
Lexington, KY
12 July 2013